Commodity Agreements and Price Stabilization

Commodity Agreements and Price Stabilization

A Policy Analysis

David L. McNicol

Lexington Books
D.C. Heath and Company
Lexington, Massachusetts
Toronto

Library of Congress Cataloging in Publication Data

McNicol, David L.
Commodity agreements and price stabilization.

Includes bibliographical references and index.
1. Commodity control. I. Title.
HF1428.M35 382.1 77-75626
ISBN 0-669-01539-3

Published simultaneously in Canada.

Printed in the United States of America.

International Standard Book Number: 0-669-01539-3

Library of Congress Catalog Card Number: 77-75626

Contents

List of Figures

List of Tables

Preface

Over the past few years, commodity agreements have become a major issue in relations between the Third World and the industrialized democracies. The less-developed countries' interest in commodities is hardly new, but there are novel elements in the current situation: the increased importance that the developed nations attach to commodities and to relations with the less-developed nations and the heavy emphasis that the less-developed nations have placed on commodity agreements as a way of restructuring the system of world trade and speeding their development.

Attention is currently focused on the Integrated Programme for Commodities (IPC), which the less-developed nations successfully advanced at the fourth United Nations Conference on Trade and Development, held in Nairobi in May 1976. The IPC, if it were established, would be based on agreements for eighteen commodities. Wherever possible, these agreements would employ buffer stocks, which would, in most cases, also involve restrictions on supply. Financing for the individual buffer stocks would be arranged through the Common Fund, which might be assigned other functions as well.

Discussion of an arrangement along the lines of the IPC generally provokes one of two reactions:

1. It is a good idea. Instability in commodity prices is a major obstacle to growth in the less-developed countries, and a system of commodity agreements would provide a badly needed vehicle for cooperation between the industrialized democracies and the nations of the Third World.
2. It is a terrible idea. The commodity agreements would attempt to increase commodity prices and would be an endless source of conflict between the developed and the less-developed nations.

Each of these reactions has some merit, but, at least as stated, both are too quick. *Commodity agreement* is a term that covers a wide variety of different arrangements that could behave in an equally wide variety of ways.

This study identifies the major types of commodity agreements and examines how they would work and what they might accomplish. The discussion of various types of commodity agreements is not carried on for its own sake but for the light that it sheds on policy problems. Through a long series of events, the developed countries have arrived at a position in which they must respond to the less-developed countries' proposals for commodity arrangements.

This study had its origins in my work as a member of the senior staff of the Council of Economic Advisors. I am indebted to Paul MacAvoy, then a member of the council, for encouraging me in this project and for suggesting directions in which it might go. I also owe debts to several individuals in the government for introducing me to various aspects of the topic, to John Lyons of American University, who was generous in his advice and criticism, and to the California Institute of Technology for providing the support, and freedom from distraction, that were so useful in the completion of the work. In the early stages of this project I received valuable research assistance from Robert Stillman and Harry Watson. Finally, I wish to thank Joyce Pilkerton, Georgeia Hutchinson, and Debra Polsky who typed successive drafts of the manuscript with great skill and good humor.

Commodity Agreements and Price Stabilization

1 The International Debate on Commodities

The heightened visibility of commodities during the past few years primarily reflects the success of the Organization of Petroleum Exporting Countries (OPEC) in quadrupling the price of oil, although the effects of the large increases in commodity prices between 1972 and 1974 and their subsequent decline also played a role. These factors, however, are of a transitory nature. The persistent source of the importance of commodity policy lies in the emergence of the Third World nations as an effective bloc. Commodity policy is now a leading issue because it has become a major element in relations between the industrialized nations (or North) and the less-developed nations (or South).

The debate on commodity problems has centered on mechanisms for stabilizing the prices of key commodities, particularly various stocking arrangements. Some of the plans considered in international discussions, however, reach much further. The more ambitious ones amount to a restructuring of world trade in commodities and of relations between the developed and less-developed nations.

The Political Context

Both the less-developed countries' (LDCs) initiatives on commodities and the developed countries' (DCs) responses have been conducted largely within the U.N. General Assembly and especially the U.N. Conference on Trade and Development (UNCTAD). UNCTAD, which is widely regarded as an organization "dedicated to exerting pressure on the advanced countries to adapt their policies to the needs of the developing countries," was established as a permanent U.N. agency in 1964.[1] In addition to its ongoing activities, every four years it convenes an international conference concerned with issues in trade and development. The first of these conferences (UNCTAD I) was held in Geneva in 1964. Since then, they have been held in 1968 (New Delhi), 1972 (Santiago), and 1976 (Nairobi).

The LDCs that attended UNCTAD I were organized, for the purposes of the conference, into the Group of 77 (G-77).[2] G-77, which has grown to include approximately 112 nations, is a descendant of the association of nonaligned nations formed in 1954 and as such reflects a profound change in the world's political geography. Most of Africa, the Indian subcontinent, and Southeast Asia were under colonial regimes when the U.N. was organized in 1945. In 1976, the

U.N. had roughly 150 member nations; Third World nations made up more than two-thirds of that total and included approximately 70 percent of the world's population.

Importance of North/South Relations

Policy on commodity trade and, more specifically, policy toward the LDCs, no longer seems so remote from domestic concerns as it did before the 1973 oil embargo. During the past few years, views in the United States on relations with the LDCs have been bound up with a fear that shortages of energy and raw materials will impose sharp constraints on economic activity in the not too distant future. Perhaps of more importance in the development of public policy were shortages of gasoline in several parts of the United States in 1974; scattered shortages of electricity and sharp rate increases during 1974 and 1975; and stringent shortages of natural gas during the winter of 1976-1977. (By "shortages," I mean that price was not allowed to rise to clear the market. The shortages that occurred reflect transitory events and effects of public policy rather than the exhaustion of natural resources.)[3] As a result of these situations, energy—and to a lesser extent raw materials supplies—has become established as an active area of government policy.

It is often taken for granted that the DCs are dependent on raw materials supplied by the LDCs and that the LDCs hold the bulk of the world's unexploited raw material resources. If this is so, and if raw materials will be persistently in shortage in the future, two conclusions follow: first, the power of the LDCs vis-à-vis the DCs has increased substantially, and, second, relations with the LDCs are of crucial importance to the DCs' economies.

The actions of OPEC seemed to provide a dramatic confirmation of these points. In October 1973, OPEC sharply reduced shipments of oil to Europe, Japan, and the United States and quadrupled the price of oil. The result has been an increase in the oil producers' revenues of some $80 billion per year and substantial economic discomfiture for oil importers among both the DCs and LDCs. The OPEC nations obviously hold significant economic and political power.

There are two other recent instances of economic actions by associations of supplying nations. The leading example is the International Bauxite Association. A second occurred during 1973 and 1974, when an organization of copper-exporting countries attempted to impose export quotas. However, a recent review of the need for supply access agreements concluded that "in most of these markets the long-run threat from restrictions appears relatively small."[4] Furthermore, there is no reason to suppose that the few examples of restrictive actions by suppliers support any statements about the other twenty to twenty-five major commodities that enter world trade.

The largest exporters of commodities, apart from oil, are the United States, Canada, and Australia. Canada and Australia export both agricultural goods and metals. The U.S. raw material exports are primarily agricultural commodities, but the country is also the world's largest producer, or among the largest producers, of iron, copper, aluminum, lead, zinc, molybdenum, vanadium, and uranium. Cobalt, tin, and tungsten are largely supplied by LDCs, but there are substitutes for these metals in most applications, substitutes for the applications in which the metals are required, and enormous room for technological development to find ways around shortages. In short, it is not accurate to say that the DCs are dependent on raw materials imported from the LDCs.

So much stress has been placed on the supply of raw materials that this conclusion might be read as implying that relations with the LDCs are unimportant, which is not the case. Relations with the LDCs are important, but for much the same reasons that they have been important throughout the postwar period. The significance of relations with them arises in part from economic concerns. The stability of supply of commodities and their prices is certainly relevant, and the DCs have an interest in maintaining access to the LDCs' economies for exports of goods and investment. Thus, the DCs have an economic interest in maintaining an open system of world trade. Conflict with the Third World works against this interest and, pushed to its limits, could disrupt trade at a large cost to the DCs.

Beyond these specific economic concerns, relations with the LDCs involve issues of international stability and national security. There is no near term prospect that any of the LDCs will pose a military threat to the United States or any other DC. Increased terrorism directed against the DCs is a possibility, and, with the spread of nuclear technology, some of the LDCs might, within perhaps a generation, develop the capability of inflicting serious damage. No one can say how this potential will evolve, but there is a presumption that the DCs' security is promoted by stable international relations and more rapid growth in the LDCs.

The LDCs are attracted to the industrialized democracies by existing trade patterns, by their need for the DCs' technology, by the sheer size of their markets, and, in many cases, by colonial ties. In addition, the DCs have accepted a responsibility for aiding the development of the LDCs. These facts, and the fact that most of the LDCs have not achieved self-sustaining growth, are also sources of friction.

The Place of Commodity Policy

The DCs and the LDCs are not divided by territorial conflicts or a struggle for military domination. North/South relations have an aspect of rivalry for political influence, but the specific issues are economic and most arise directly from the fact that the DCs and the LDCs are trading partners.

The major items on the agenda of North/South relations are stabilization of commodity prices via international commodity agreements; reduction of tariff and nontariff barriers that limit the LDCs' access to the DCs' markets; development assistance; international monetary arrangements, including rescheduling the LDCs' external debt and means for helping the LDCs cover balance of payments deficits; transfer of technology and, specifically, the international patent system; regulation of the activities of multinational corporations; and the law of the sea, especially control of deep-sea mining operations. Although all of these topics are important, commodity agreements have become the central issue in North/South relations at least in the view of the LDCs.

The LDCs' position on commodities is associated with an analytical tradition concerned with the relationship between trade and development. It is argued that the terms of trade have shifted against commodities and in favor of manufactures and that this trend can be expected to continue. To the extent that this is the case, earnings from the export of commodities will be insufficient to pay for the imports required for development. That can clearly be justification for foreign aid as well as for commodity agreements. A second argument, which points somewhat more directly to intervention in the commodity markets, is that instability in commodity prices and export earnings is a major obstacle to development.

The attitude that the LDCs bring to commodity problems is largely explained by these arguments and the example provided by OPEC. However, the debate on commodity arrangements has been shaped more by impasses that have been reached on other issues than by analyses of the role of trade in development.

Insofar as relations with the LDCs were concerned, the two decades after World War II were the era of foreign aid. The Marshall Plan, which was inaugurated in 1947, was of unprecedented size and scope, and because it was highly successful, it became a model. A variety of bilateral programs for the LDCs—the Marshall Plan was aimed solely at Europe—was developed, and later the emphasis began to shift toward multilateral aid programs.

Development assistance programs have not succeeded in producing self-sustaining growth in the LDCs, primarily because of the structure of existing programs, too little funding, and limitations on injections of capital as a stimulus to development.[5] Although some of these problems could be overcome, it is generally conceded that the current spending on development assistance is much less than would be required to provide rapid economic growth in the LDCs and that the political situation in the DCs is such that development assistance will not increase significantly. This is a pivotal point. Both the plans advanced by the LDCs and the DCs' responses are cast against existing limitations of development assistance.

Tariff and nontariff barriers to trade are a second, and equally important, issue. From the LDCs' perspective, tariff and nontariff barriers to trade are one of the dominant features of the current system of world trade. Agricultural exports from the LDCs are constrained by tariffs and quotas designed to protect the DCs' domestic producers (U.S. sugar quotas are an example).[6] The development of the metals industries in the LDCs is limited by "tariff escalation," which refers to increases in the tariff with the degree of processing. For example, the DCs' tariffs on copper ore and concentrate and refined copper are low (zero in some cases) while their tariffs on semifabricated copper products are typically in the range of 10-25 percent ad valorem.[7] This makes it more difficult for LDCs that produce copper to create domestic semifabricating industries.

The Kennedy Round (1963-1967) of negotiations held under the auspices of the General Agreement on Tariffs and Trade (GATT) resulted in reductions in the tariff and nontariff barriers faced by the LDCs.[8] Some modest revisions have been made since then, but the prospects for the proposals for larger reductions do not seem encouraging. The major obstacle lies in the domestic politics of the DCs. Lowering a tariff or nontariff barrier to trade does immediate harm to the protected industry, and this naturally generates political opposition.

The United States has argued that international cooperation on development should focus on development assistance and the reduction in tariff and nontariff barriers to trade and measures to increase the flows of private capital to the LDCs. Since little progress has been made in these areas, it is understandable that the LDCs would come to see direct action on commodities as a more fruitful avenue to explore. The checks on development assistance and reduction of barriers to trade imposed by their domestic politics also constrain the DCs' options, and they have strong reasons for responding to the LDCs' concerns. Both sides are, then, led to focus attention on commodity problems.

Proposed Commodity Arrangements

There is nothing new about the idea of creating international agencies to intervene in world commodity markets; this possibility was considered at the Versailles Conference in 1919.[9] No actions on commodities were adopted at that time, and there seems to have been virtually no multilateral involvement by the DCs in the commodity markets during the 1920s. Several commodity agreements were, however, formed during the 1930s, and commodity problems were a fairly active area of governmental concern.

By far the best-known proposal that emerged during this period was made by John Maynard Keynes in a 1942 memorandum to the United Kingdom Treasury. Keynes was concerned with "meaningless short-period price swings" and with the business cycle. He argued that "the same technique of Buffer Stocks, which has to be called into being to deal with the former problem, is also capable of making a large contribution to the cure of the Trade Cycle itself."[10] The idea that buffer stocks (organizations that buy or sell as necessary to hold prices within established bounds) have an important role to play in dealing with the problems of unemployment and inflation has never gained much popularity. In fact, it seems a bit out of place in terms of modern macroeconomics. The rationale that Keynes offered for his proposal is perhaps less important than the proposal itself.

Keynes suggested a series of buffer stocks, each operated by a commodity control, and a general council for commodity controls. The general council would review individual commodity controls before they were established to ensure that each conformed to preestablished principles, review the commodity controls' operations, and make policy recommendations to them. Finally, Keynes suggested that the buffer stocks be financed by the International Clearing Union, which was a proposed institution along the lines of what became the International Monetary Fund (IMF).

While Keynes's proposal was not picked up, there was some interest in commodity agreements in the early postwar years (for example, chapter VI of the Havana Charter, which set out guidelines on commodity agreements).[11] However, the interest in commodity agreements was short-lived, and it was not until UNCTAD I in 1964 that commodities began to emerge as a major issue. Commodity arrangements became increasingly important in successive UNCTADs and were the central issue of UNCTAD IV held in Nairobi in May 1976.

The LDCs' proposals on commodity arrangements evolved through three distinct phases. The point of departure was the case-by-case approach to commodity agreements. The resolution adopted by UNCTAD I that dealt with commodities specified that agreements should be reached on a case-by-case basis and went on to create the Commission on Commodity Arrangements and Policies as part of the permanent machinery of UNCTAD. The commission was directed to "help arrange negotiations in conformity with the general objectives and principles set forth" within two years.[12]

The United States rejected the possibility of any "grand design for the myriad of individual commodity situations and problems" but accepted the case-by-case approach.[13] This position was nothing new, for before UNCTAD I the United States had been a member of International Wheat Agreements, the Inter-American Coffee Agreement, the International Coffee Agreement, and International Sugar Agreements. However, although it accepted the case-by-case approach, the United States clearly had no enthusiasm for commodity agreements and took the position that the basis for international cooperation and development lay elsewhere.

If the decisions made at UNCTAD I had been effective, several commodity agreements would have been set up by the time UNCTAD II convened four years later in New Delhi. The fact that no major agreements were created between

1964 and 1968 was reflected in resolution 16 (II), which called for the beginning, renewal, or continuation of negotiations on agreements on five commodities or groups of commodities and the strengthening of an informal agreement reached for jute.[14] The resolution was adopted unanimously. Much more controversial was the idea of an integrated policy on commodity agreements, such as that in chapter VI of the Havana Charter. The proposal was not for an integrated program, which emerged later, but for a statement of the sorts of techniques and organizational structures that would be generally acceptable.[15] Adherence to a charter of this sort would not commit a nation to an agreement in any particular commodity, but it would imply a presumption in favor of any agreement that met the charter's standards.

The U.S. position on commodity agreements at UNCTAD II was essentially the same as it had been at UNCTAD I. It rejected the notion of an integrated commodity policy but accepted the case-by-case approach and pointed to its participation in negotiations on agreements for coffee and sugar.[16]

Between UNCTAD II and UNCTAD III, held in Santiago in 1972, the idea of an integrated policy on commodity agreements had come very close to becoming an integrated program on commodities. Resolution 54 (III) recommended that:

1. The International Bank for Reconstruction and Development (IBRD) should act to facilitate the conclusion of agreements for stabilizing prices of certain commodities.
2. The World Bank Group should make price stabilization an object of its loan policies.
3. The IBRD should act with the IMF in financing stocking and diversification programs.
4. The World Bank Group should provide direct financing to international agencies whose objective is to stabilize the prices of raw materials in accordance with agreements on individual commodities.
5. The World Bank Group should systematically assist in the diversification of production.[17]

The United States voted against resolution 54 (III), and most of the other DCs apparently abstained.[18]

After UNCTAD III, proposals for commodity arrangements became bound up with what was to be called the "new international economic order." *Economic order* in part refers to the existing distribution of income. In this sense, the existing economic order is characterized by the fact that 70 percent of the world's population lives in the LDCs while these people obtain only 30 percent of the world's income. A new order would be a situation in which income was much more evenly distributed. *Economic order* is also used to refer to the markets, trade barriers, government policies, and international institutions that make up the existing system of world trade.

The LDCs successfully pressed for the adoption of the Declaration on the Establishment of a New International Economic Order at the 1974 U.N. General Assembly Special Session on Raw Materials and Development. This special session also approved the Program of Action on the Establishment of a New International Economic Order, which directed the UNCTAD Secretariat to design measures along the lines set forth in the resolution.[19] In response, the UNCTAD Secretariat developed the Integrated Programme for Commodities (IPC), which the LDCs regard as the principal vehicle for obtaining the new international economic order.

The IPC envisions the creation of agreements for each of eighteen commodities. (Agreements would initially be reached for ten core commodities: cocoa, coffee, tea, sugar, cotton, jute, sisal, rubber, copper, and tin. The other eight commodities are bananas, bauxite, iron ore, manganese, meat, phosphates, tropical timber, and vegetable oils.) Whenever possible, these agreements would be built around a buffer stock. The individual international commodity organizations would be related by the Common Fund, which would have three functions: to finance the buffer stocks, to trade on its own account in certain limited circumstances, and to provide loans or grants to aid the LDCs in diversifying their economies.

The general similarity between the IPC and Keynes's proposal is obvious; the differences, though no less real, are less apparent. Keynes drew a careful distinction between restrictive schemes, designed to increase price above its long-run competitive level, and arrangements designed only to reduce price fluctuations. The former he identified with restrictions on production and the latter with buffer stocks. Keynes felt that the use of export controls might sometimes be "a necessary accompaniment of stabilization," but he rejected "chronic, as distinct from temporary, restriction," and he built into his proposal a number of safeguards to ensure that the buffer stocks' target prices would be appropriately adjusted.[20] The IPC neither clearly honors nor entirely rejects these rules. In some cases its commodity agreements would allow the use of export quotas only in "emergency situations," but in others, export quotas and/or production controls would be used on a permanent basis. The documents that describe the IPC also at least leave open the possibility that the agreements would attempt to increase commodity prices.

The debate on commodity arrangements reached a turning point—presumably not the last—at UNCTAD IV when the plenary session adopted a resolution on commodities which laid down a timetable for the creation of what would effectively be the Integrated Programme.[21]

Perspectives on the Issues

Discussion of an arrangement along the lines of the IPC generally provokes one of two reactions:

1. It is a terrible idea. Commodity agreements invariably attempt to increase prices, which is against the interests of importing nations and is an inefficient way of transferring income to the LDCs. In addition, commodity agreements generally do not work and involve the politicization of world trade.
2. It is a good idea. Reducing fluctuations in commodity prices would remove a major obstacle to the LDCs' growth and is an excellent way for the DCs to redeem the commitment they have assumed to aid the LDCs' development. Additionally, commodity agreements, as cooperative ventures, would tend to improve relations between the DCs and the LDCs.

While many would find it easy to choose between these views, neither can be quickly and simply established as definitely correct. They are useful, however, because they evoke in summary form the major elements of a complex issue. They point first of all to the relevant criteria. One criterion is the direct economic self-interest of importing nations; a second, which arises because the DCs have assumed some responsibility for helping the LDCs develop, is effects on the LDCs' growth; a third is that there is a concern with the character of North/South relations. There is no disagreement that these—and not East/West relations—are the primary considerations.

There are, of course, disagreements among individuals and nations over the weight that should be assigned to different criteria, but these are not worth exploring because they do not shed much light on the controversy. Within the DCs, disputes over the role, if any, that should be assigned to commodity agreements do not revolve around differences in political values.

Some broad, factual questions involving the commodities markets are a source of genuine disagreement. One of these is the extent of the DCs' dependence on raw materials supplied by the LDCs. A closely related question is the extent of the danger that raw materials will be cartelized or that raw materials supply will be periodically subject to severe disruptions. A third issue is the extent to which reducing price fluctuations would speed the LDCs' development. These and several other questions on the same plane are important but not in themselves determinative. There is no set of factual questions about the commodity markets that, if resolved, would require reasonable people to agree on the proper place of commodity arrangements.

This is in part so because of a disagreement over whether commodity agreements should be used as a means of transferring income to the LDCs. The United States has consistently rejected the use of commodity agreements as a transfer mechanism, but this position is not accepted by the LDCs or shared by all of the DCs. An example is a statement issued by the French government in 1972: "By making consumers in rich countries pay a higher price for these food stuffs and metals than would result from the free play of competition, France is fostering the most acceptable form of aid-payment for human effort rather than charity pure and simple."[22] More to the point, perhaps, is the fact that direct transfers require governmental appropriations, while the costs of higher prices are borne by consumers generally and so are less visible.

Price increases are known to be an inefficient way of making transfers, and they are an administrative and political nightmare, even when compared with foreign aid programs. Any argument in favor of using price increases to transfer income to the LDCs must then be made on a political basis. First, it can be argued that price increases are the only politically feasible means of making transfers and that the imperatives—moral or otherwise—for transferring resources to the LDCs override the inefficiency of using price increases to do the job.[23] Second, by making concessions to the LDCs on commodity prices, the DCs might obtain offsetting political gains. In its most substantial form, this argument sees commodity agreements as cooperative ventures that would tend to bind the DCs and the LDCs into a community of interest.

Discussions of commodity agreements would be relatively simple if the question were only whether they should be used to make transfers via higher prices. There is, however, some interest in using commodity agreements only to reduce fluctuations in commodity prices, but this distinction is in itself a major source of controversy; for example, position 1 can be associated with one type of arrangement and position 2 with another, both of which fall under the general heading "commodity agreement."

The major building blocks of commodity agreements are buffer stocks, export quotas, and production controls. A buffer stock might be operated without restrictions on supply; or restrictions on supply might be used without a buffer stock; or a buffer stock and controls on supply can be used together. Controls on supply could be triggered automatically in certain circumstances or used only if accepted by a majority of importing nations. The operating rules of a buffer stock can also be set up in various ways. Anyone familiar with these mechanisms can easily design dozens of different types of commodity arrangements, and in most cases it is not obvious whether the arrangement would only reduce price fluctuations or increase the average level of prices. In fact, this simple dichotomy does not capture all of the possibilities. A commodity agreement may attempt to increase prices and fail. Or it may be intended to reduce price fluctuations and actually magnify them or be led by flaws in its rules into attempting to increase the average level of price. Moreover, a commodity agreement is not simply a bit of clockwork. It must focus suppliers' interest in higher prices and present the possibility of conflict among its member nations. Inevitably, then, the creation of a commodity agreement will to some degree politicize what are otherwise economic issues to be handled by individual buyers and sellers as they choose.

Concluding Comments

It is possible to describe, using standard methods and results, what various types of commodity arrangements could accomplish, what economic pressures would be placed on them, and what conflicts would arise. This information provides a basis for analyzing how an integrated system of commodity agreements would function and whether it would be stable. That, in brief, is the program of the remainder of this book. The overall aims of succeeding chapters, which explore several byways, are to distinguish sharply agreements designed to increase prices from those designed to reduce price fluctuations and to assess the relevant characteristics of each type of agreement.

A discussion along these lines cannot fully resolve disputes over commodity agreements, but it may be helpful. Decisions on whether to create a system of commodity agreements must be based on broad considerations of political purpose, but the concrete choices must be made at the level of particular arrangements. Examination of alternative types of commodity agreements can thus serve to indicate what policy choices are available.

Notes

1. I. Frank, "The Role of Trade in Development," in R. Gardner and M. Millikan, eds. *The Global Partnership: International Agencies and Economic Development* (New York: Praeger, 1968), p. 70.

2. Although its members have shown a remarkable degree of cohesion, G-77 is not an alliance or even a formally established organization. It is perhaps best understood as a political party. It has taken the lead in obtaining a consensus among the LDCs and in advancing proposals of interest to them. See Frederick Strauss, "Report of the United Nations Conference on Trade and Development," mimeo. (U.S. Department of Commerce, Bureau of International Commerce, July 1964), pp. 10-12, 52, for a discussion of G-77's role in UNCTAD I.

3. See P.W. MacAvoy and R.S. Pindyck, *The Economics of the Natural Gas Shortage* (Amsterdam: North-Holland Publishing Company, 1975), esp. chaps. 1, 5.

4. Charles River Associates, "Economic Issues Underlying Supply Access Agreements: A General Analysis and Prospects in 10 Mineral Markets," report to the U.S. Department of Labor, Bureau of International Labor Affairs, July 1975, p. 6-3.

5. See Robert E. Asher, *Development Assistance in the Seventies* (Washington, D.C.: The Brookings Institution, 1970), esp. chap. 3.

6. See Ilse Mintz, *U.S. Import Quotas: Costs and Consequences* (Washington, D.C.: American Enterprise Institute, 1973), chap. 4, for a discussion of costs associated with U.S. sugar import quotas. UNCTAD, *Proceedings of the United Nations Conference on Trade and Development, Second Session: Commodity Problems and Policies*, TD/97, vol. 2 (New York: United Nations, 1968), pp. 85-97, lists tariff and nontariff barriers to imports of major commodities into the United States, the United Kingdom, the European Economic Commu-

nity, and Japan. See Ingo Walter, "Barriers to International Competition: The Application and Liberalization of Nontariff Distortions," in *The United States and International Markets,* ed. Robert C. Hawkins and Ingo Walter (Lexington, Mass.: Lexington Books, 1972), for estimates of nontariff barriers in the DCs on the LDCs' trade.

7. Political and Economic Planning Committee, *Atlantic Tariffs and Trade* (London: Allen and Unwin, 1962). The Kennedy Round produced only minor changes in the structure of copper tariffs.

8. See John W. Evans, *The Kennedy Round in American Trade Policy* (Cambridge: Harvard University Press, 1971), chap. 15.

9. See Benjamin B. Wallace and Lynn R. Edminster, *International Control of Raw Materials* (Washington, D.C.: The Brookings Institution, 1930), pp. 318-322, and the introduction to International Labor Office, *Intergovernmental Commodity Control Agreements* (Montreal: International Labor Office, 1943), for reviews of international discussions of commodity problems during the 1920s and 1930s. In the years just after World War I, concern was apparently focused on what would now be called supply access problems.

10. J.M. Keynes, "The International Control of Raw Materials," *Journal of International Economics* 4 (1974):305. See also Keynes, "The Policy of Government Storage of Foodstuffs and Raw Materials," *Economic Journal* 45 (1938):449-460.

11. See Herman Walker, "The International Law of Commodity Agreements," *Law and Contemporary Problems* 28 (Spring 1963):400-403, for a discussion of chapter VI of the Havana Charter and its relationship to GATT. The Havana Charter never entered into force.

12. UNCTAD, *Trade and Development: Final Act and Report*, E/CONF. 46/141 (New York: United Nations, 1964), paragraph 14, p. 28.

13. Statement of Undersecretary of State George W. Ball in UNCTAD, *Trade and Development: Policy Statements*, E/CONF. 46/141 (New York: United Nations, 1964), p. 396.

14. UNCTAD, *Proceedings of the United Nations Conference on Trade and Development, Second Session: Report and Annexes*, TD/97, vol. 1 (New York: United Nations, 1968), pp. 34-36.

15. UNCTAD, *Proceedings: Commodity Problems,* pp. 1-67, was a study of an integrated commodity policy. The resolution calling for comments on the idea of an integrated commodity policy was adopted without dissent. UNCTAD, *Proceedings: Report and Annexes,* p. 36. However, most of the DCs were apparently not in favor of an integrated commodity policy. UNCTAD, *Proceedings: Report and Annexes*, paragraph 17, p. 234.

16. See the summary of the statement made by Undersecretary of State Eugene V. Rostow, UNCTAD, *Proceedings: Report and Annexes,* pp. 189-192, esp. paragraphs 15-17.

17. UNCTAD, *Proceedings of the United Nations Conference on Trade and*

Development, Third Session: Report and Annexes, TD/180, vol. 1 (New York: United Nations, 1973), pp. 78-80.

18. Ibid., p. 134.

19. The two resolutions were combined in the Charter of Economic Rights and Duties of State, which was approved by the General Assembly in December 1974. The Charter on the Economic Rights and Duties of States was also adopted at UNCTAD II as resolution 45 (III). See ibid., pp. 58-59.

20. Keynes, "International Control," p. 299.

21. The United States reserved its position on the Common Fund but voted for the resolution. See U.S., Congress, *Report by Congressional Advisors to UNCTAD IV* (Washington, D.C.: Government Printing Office, 1976), pp. 191-193, for the U.S. statement of reservation and interpretation.

22. Quoted by Z. Mikdashi, "Collusion Could Work," *Foreign Policy* 14 (Spring 1974):59.

23. See Richard N. Cooper, "A New International Economic Order for Mutual Gain," *Foreign Policy* 26 (Spring 1977):65-120, for a lucid discussion of the major ethical arguments associated with the use of commodity agreements as a transfer mechanism.

2 Economic Objectives and Stabilization Mechanisms

Buffer stocks are popularly described as a means of speeding the LDCs' development by stabilizing commodity prices. These words are simply a slogan and not a very informative one at that. To some, *price stabilization* means a reduction in price fluctuations without an increase in the average level of prices; to others, it means a reduction in price fluctuations and an increase in commodity prices. There is a connection between price stabilization in each of these senses and economic development, but they imply very different types of commodity arrangements.

Although disagreements over whether commodity agreements should be used to increase prices cannot be easily resolved, a measure of agreement on what means are appropriate to alternative objectives should be obtainable. This is possible since it would be generally accepted that, given the objective, the least costly means should be used. Agreement on the correspondence of objectives and means, of course, would not end disagreement over objectives, but it does provide a useful bridge from broad principles to specific measures.

Instability in Commodity Prices and the LDCs' Export Earnings

It is commonly assumed that the LDCs obtain most of their export earnings by selling commodities to the DCs, that commodity prices are subject to large fluctuations, and that the export earnings of LDCs are extremely unstable. The facts are somewhat more complicated, but these views are substantially correct.

The data presented in table 2-1 indicate that most LDCs derive the bulk of their export earnings from only a few commodities. Only one of these nations (British West Indies) is based on a one-crop economy, but more than half of the LDCs derive at least 50 percent of their export earnings from three or fewer commodities, and only 18 of the 114 LDCs obtain less than 10 percent of their export earnings from three commodities.

Table 2-2 provides information bearing on the importance of commodity exports in the LDCs' economies. Export earnings were at least 40 percent of gross domestic product (GDP) for twenty-five of the LDCs in 1972. Most of the nations in this group have classic few-crop economies (that is, their export earnings are derived from only a few commodities, and the export sector is a large part of the economy). This is not, however, typical of LDCs as a group.

Table 2-1
Percent of the LDCs' Export Earnings Derived from Commodities, Except Petroleum

Percent of Export Earnings	*Largest Commodity Export*		*Largest Three Commodity Exports*		*All Commodity Exports*	
	Number	*Cumulative*	*Number*	*Cumulative*	*Number*	*Cumulative*
90-100	1	1	6	6	12	12
80-90	4	5	5	11	12	24
70-80	4	9	6	17	15	39
60-70	6	15	11	28	13	52
50-60	12	27	15	43	12	64
40-50	7	34	10	53	9	73
30-40	12	46	11	64	9	82
20-30	18	64	11	75	9	91
10-20	15	79	7	82	5	96
0-10	35	114	32	114	18	114

Source: Compiled from data in International Bank for Reconstruction and Development, *Commodity Trade and Price Trends* (1975).

Export earnings were less than 40 percent of GDP for eighty-seven of the LDCs and less than 20 percent for sixty of the LDCs.

The commodities industries are subject to inherent uncertainties to a greater extent than manufacturing or services. Weather is the principal source of uncertainty for agricultural commodites. There are also wide swings in demand for metals, although their supplies are reasonably stable. Furthermore, because the short-run supply and demand for most commodities are price inelastic, small variations in either supply or demand give rise to relatively large changes in price.

Measures of the variations in the prices of fifteen commodities are given in table 2-3 along with similar data for the U.S. prices of several manufactured goods. An examination of the highs and lows clearly suggests that commodity prices are much less stable than the prices of manufactured goods, an impression that is confirmed by the coefficients of variation.[1] For the 1951-1975 period, the coefficients of variation for the commodity prices (except for bananas, wheat, and rice) were at least twice those of the manufactured goods.

Since a relatively small fraction of the LDCs' exports are of manufactures, these facts suggest that the LDCs' export earnings are less stable than those of the DCs. Some early studies found the LDCs' export earnings to be only slightly more unstable than those of the DCs, but more recent work indicates that the difference is large. In particular Erb and Schiavo-Campo found that the mean value of their index of instability for the LDCs was about 30 percent above that

Table 2-2
Distribution of the LDCs' Export Earnings as a Percent of Gross Domestic Product, 1972

Export Earnings as a Percent of GDP	*Number of LDCs*	*Cumulative*
100	3	3
80-100	4	7
60-80	10	17
40-60	8	25
20-40	27	52
10-20	35	87
0-10	25	112

Sources: International Bank for Reconstruction and Development, *Commodity Trade and Price Trends* (1975); Europa Publishing Company, *Europa Yearbook* (1975); and International Monetary Fund, *International Financial Statistics* (1974).

Note: In several cases, it was necessary to use the average value of exports for 1971-1972.

for the DCs during the 1946-1958 period and more than twice that of the DCs during the 1954-1966 period.[2]

The facts presented in tables 2-1 and 2-3 do not necessarily imply that the LDCs' export earnings will be less stable than those of the DCs. The obstacle to arriving at this conclusion lies in the fact that diversification reduces instability to the extent that the individual components of a sum are negatively correlated and increases instability to the extent that they are positively correlated. Hence, the exports of a country can be concentrated in only a few products, each of which is unstable, while the country's overall export earnings are relatively stable. Nevertheless, the LDCs' export earnings are relatively unstable. Thus, taking the statistical properties of the component series as given, most individual LDC's exports are concentrated in small numbers of products, earnings from which tend to move together.[3]

It is possible to proceed from this point to ask why the statistical properties of the series are as they are by investigating the relationship between measures of instability in the LDCs' export earnings and other variables (geographic concentration of exports, product concentration, and so forth). But while the results of such exercises are important for some purposes, they need not be pursued here.[4]

Basis for Stabilization Arrangements

In the international sphere, more than in the domestic, the existence of an economic problem does not in itself constitute a case for action. This is to say that

Table 2-3
Variation in Commodity Prices, 1951-1975

Commodity	*High*	*Low*	*Coefficient of Variation*
	(1975 = 100)		
Cocoa	190.7	54.9	0.29
Coffee	288.2	100.0	.25
Tea	274.2	100.0	.26
Sugar	128.7	16.9	.61
Cotton	227.1	100.0	.22
Jute[a]	166.7	77.4	.21
Sisal[b]	144.5	41.4	.38
Rubber	531.6	100.0	.38
Copper	285.3	100.0	.33
Tin	129.0	67.9	.20
Bananas	214.1	100.0	.18
Beef[c]	129.4	26.8	.55
Rice	153.5	69.2	.21
Wheat	125.6	72.9	.14
Wool	324.7	100.0	.29
Electrical machinery and equipment	127.0	100.0	.06
Mechanical power and transmission equipment	103.0	74.3	.10
New cars[d]	153.2	100.0	.13
Women's and girls' apparel	140.8	100.0	.08

Sources: International Bank for Reconstruction and Development, *Commodity Trade and Price Trends* (1975); United Nations, Food and Agriculture Organization, *Trade Yearbook* (1974); United Nations, *Monthly Bulletin of Statistics*, March, 1976; U.S. Department of Labor, Bureau of Labor Statistics, *Consumer Prices and Price Indices* (various issues); Bureau of Labor Statistics, *Wholesale Prices and Price Indexes* (various issues).

Note: Commodity prices were deflated by the U.N. world price index for all commodities. The prices of electrical machinery and equipment and mechanical power and transmission equipment were deflated by the U.S. wholesale price index of durable manufactures. The prices of new cars and women's and girls' apparel were deflated by the U.S. consumer price index.

[a]Series begins with 1954.

[b]Series begins with 1955.

[c]Series ends with 1974.

[d]Series begins with 1953.

an argument for commodity agreements cannot be made simply in terms of facts about fluctuations in commodity prices and the LDCs' export earnings but must proceed from some recognized basis for international cooperation. The range of choice is limited to humanitarian concerns, security, mutual advantage of the contracting parties, and economic development. Of these, economic development is the obvious candidate because the DCs have assumed a commitment to help the LDCs develop. This commitment is neither unlimited in magnitude nor indiscriminate in means, but it would be generally conceded that, to the extent that instability of prices or export earnings impinges on the growth of the LDCs, there is reason to consider measures directed to the commodity markets.

Commodity Trade and Development

No one doubts that trade in commodities is of vital importance to the LDCs. The sectors devoted to commodity exports are virtually the entire economy in some of the LDCs, and, for the LDCs generally, commodity exports are the principal source of foreign exchange and hence a major determinant of their ability to purchase the imports required for development. But beyond this broad descriptive level, there are differences of opinion on the respect in which the role of commodities in the LDCs' economies provides a case for commodity agreements.

The LDCs' Terms of Trade. One prominent position is cast against the question of whether the exchange earnings that the LDCs can obtain from commodities trade are sufficient to support their development. Dr. Raúl Prebish, first secretary-general of UNCTAD, is the leading proponent of the view that it is not. He argues that the terms of trade in the past have moved against commodities in favor of manufactures and that this trend can be expected to persist. If so, the ability of the LDCs to purchase the imports required for development will decline over time.[5] Prebisch's conclusion was in part based on theoretical arguments and in part on observed trends in the LDCs' terms of trade. Neither aspect of the argument has withstood subsequent examination. In particular, there does not seem to be a persistent tendency for the LDCs' terms of trade to deteriorate.[6] These criticisms need not be pursued, however, because there is a sense in which the policy implications of Prebish's argument are generally accepted.

How rapid a rate of growth in the LDCs is rapid enough is a political judgment and not a matter of how the world trading system works. It is possible to argue that the commodities trade provides some of the financing required for growth—and that the system would do even better if trade barriers were reduced—without assuming that market forces provide sufficiently rapid growth.

The DCs (especially the United States) have adopted positions roughly along these lines. On the one hand, the United States has generally favored reductions in trade barriers and stressed the role of private capital in development. On the other hand, it and the other DCs have made transfers to the LDCs through development assistance programs, which is to admit implicitly that the rate of development provided by market forces is insufficiently rapid.

From this perspective, the crucial connection between trade in commodities and economic development does not lie in price or earnings instability but in the position of the LDCs in the commodity markets. The model is OPEC, which has had a tremendous effect on the development of the major oil producers among the LDCs. But this effect was not achieved by reducing fluctuations in oil prices but by quadrupling them.

Instability and Development. Whatever position is taken on price increases as a means of transferring income to the LDCs, discussion of economic development as a basis for commodity agreements is not concluded. There is a second and much more widely accepted argument, which holds that periodic, drastic declines in the LDCs' export earnings are a significant obstacle to development.

Effects on government planning are often offered as the link between sharp declines in export earnings and development; for example, "I could hardly think of any planner in a developing country whose plans have not gone awry because of the frequent, and sometimes unexpected, aberrations that occur in the commodity markets."[7] The force of this argument turns on the fact that most of the LDCs have a tremendous demand for infrastructure investment—roads, hospitals, schools—which is the responsibility of the government. The government also assumes a substantial responsibility for agricultural and industrial investment in many of the LDCs.

Both sorts of investments require manufactured goods, and imports of these items must be paid for with foreign currencies, which the LDCs acquire largely by the export of commodities. Governments can tap the flow of foreign exchange earnings in a variety of ways. One procedure, which is common in the agricultural industries, is to require producers to sell to a government marketing board at a price set well below the market price. Payment is made in the national currency. The government then sells the commodity in international markets and is paid in foreign currencies.

Whatever method is used, the foreign exchange available to the LDCs' governments depends on commodity prices. When commodity prices are high, the government's command over foreign exchange is correspondingly high. A sharp drop in commodity prices results in a decline in export earnings and government revenues. (This statement assumes that the demand for commodities is price inelastic, which seems to be the case generally. See table A-1.) If imports are maintained at existing levels, a reduction in the value of exports produces a balance-of-payments deficit, which puts pressure on the country's exchange rate and creates a demand for loans. Borrowing from international agencies and private sources can temporarily take the place of export earnings, but eventually imports must be cut back, and, to the extent that they depend on imports, development programs are disrupted.

The effects of declines in export earnings on the LDCs' governments are only part of the problem, and perhaps not the most important part. The statement that "instability in export earnings is a major obstacle to development" is often used as a metaphor for a complex set of events. A sharp decline in the price of a commodity can cause corresponding declines in individual producers' incomes, cutbacks in production, and unemployment, and these in turn can lead to more general types of political and social disruption. In effect, the argument is that, for a few-crop economy, a decline in price constitutes a situation analogous to a major depression in the United States.

The logic of these and other reasonable arguments that show how instability in export earnings can be an obstacle to development is not a major source of contention.[8] There is, however, disagreement about the magnitude and extent of the problem. McBean found a negative correlation between growth in GNP and instability in export earnings for a sample of eleven LDCs.[9] However, the correlations did not differ significantly from zero, which means that this test indicates the absence of any marked effect of instability in export earnings on GNP. Furthermore, on each of several tests, the relationship between investment and instability proved to be statistically insignificant, but higher levels of investment were associated with less stable export earnings. Knudsen and Parnes also found a positive association between investment and instability in export earnings and a positive association between the rate of growth of GNP and GNP per capita and instability in export earnings.[10]

The results of several other studies partially contradict these results. Maizels pointed out several statistical flaws in McBean's study and showed that, with minor changes, the data gave a positive correlation between GNP and instability in export earnings.[11] Massell, Pearson, and Fitch also found that export earnings were positively correlated with imports, investments, and GNP.[12] More recently, Rangarajan and Sundararajan, using small economic models for eleven countries, found that in five cases predicted GNP grows more rapidly when exports are stable than it does when exports fluctuate.[13]

The mixed nature of the results obtained by these studies is not surprising in view of the wide differences that exist among the LDCs, and the studies should be read in that light. It seems reasonable to conclude that available studies refute the proposition that instability in export earnings is a crucial problem for all of the LDCs and also refute the notion that instability in export earnings is not a significant obstacle to development for some LDCs. Although it is not clear where the line should be drawn, the weight of the evidence seems to be that instability is a major problem for many, and perhaps a majority, of the LDCs.

Gains to Buyers from Price Stabilization

Economic development would in some respect be the primary basis for commodity agreements, but it is not the only consideration. Buyers can also gain from a reduction in the fluctuations in commodity prices, and, to the extent that they do, commodity agreements have an aspect of mutual advantage to buyers and sellers. The suggestion that there are gains to the DCs from reducing price fluctuations may seem unimportant. These gains are certainly not highly visible, and they are never offered as a major reason for creating commodity agreements. However, the argument that there are gains to the DCs from price stabilization plays an important role in discussions of what type of arrangements might be appropriate.

Inflation. Perhaps the most frequently made argument is that increases in commodity prices are a significant cause of inflation in the DCs. These increases cause increases in costs of production, and so tend to produce increases in final product prices and eventually wages. Decreases in commodity prices tend to work in the other direction, but it is asserted that because the final product price and wages are rigid downward increases in commodity prices are built into the structure of the DCs' economies.

There are several other, and much more important, causes of inflation: expansion of the money supply; excess demand, whether caused by government deficits or autonomous increases in spending; and wage push inflation. Laying aside criticisms of the argument, then, the question is whether increases in commodity prices are a significant source of inflation.[14]

Although careful empirical analyses of this issue are unavailable, it seems unlikely that increases in the prices of imported commodities are an important source of inflation in the United States. In 1975, GNP in the United States was $1,516.3 billion, while the value of imports from all LDCs except petroleum exporting nations was $17.8 billion, or 1.2 percent of GNP.[15] Simply on this basis, it is implausible to suppose that the prices of imported commodities could have much impact on final product prices in the United States.

Effects on Cost. A less complicated argument concerns the effects of price fluctuations on the costs incurred by both buyers and sellers. Increases in the magnitude of price fluctuations tend to increase costs in three ways. First, as the degree of price instability increases, both buyers and sellers may be led to employ more working capital and hold larger inventories. Second, price instability can increase costs by requiring changes in production rates, creating problems of scheduling the work force, complicating purchasing decisions, and so forth. Third, instability in prices typically implies instability in suppliers' returns, and, as returns become more variable, the cost of capital to suppliers increases.

These costs are real enough, but there is some question about the magnitude of cost savings that would result from reducing price fluctuations. In most of the commodity industries, working capital requirements are relatively low, and the agricultural industries are typically not capital intensive. Furthermore, if a buffer stock is employed, at least much of any reduction of buyers' and sellers' inventories would simply be transferred to the buffer stock. To the extent that this occurs, total inventory costs would not fall.[16] These considerations suggest that cost reductions would be minor.

Effects on Expenditures and Profit. There is no doubt that measures to reduce price fluctuations would have an impact on buyers' expenditures and suppliers' revenues and thereby on profits. Buyers gain during a period of shortage if a commodity agreement can sell to maintain price below what it would be otherwise; suppliers gain when steps are taken to support price. But the other side of these facts is that, compared to a situation of no intervention, buyers lose when price is supported, and suppliers lose when price is held down. There is, then, a question of the net advantage to buyers and sellers of reducing price fluctuations.

Table 2-4 presents a hypothetical example focusing on buyers' expenditures. It is assumed that the quantity demanded is independent of price but varies, with the business cycle, from low (80) to normal (100) to high (120). Supply is assumed to be stable and to have an elasticity of 0.3. The first set of figures in

Table 2-4
Example of the Effects of Price Stabilization on Buyers' Expenditures When Supply Is Stable and Demand Varies

Without Price Stabilization

Supply	*Demand*	*Price*	*Expenditure*
120	120	1.67	200.00
100	100	1.00	100.00
80	80	0.33	26.67
			326.67

With Price Stabilization

Supply	*Buffer Stock Purchases (+) and Sales (–)*	*Demand*	*Price*	*Expenditure*
100	20	120	1.00	120.00
100	0	100	1.00	100.00
100	–20	80	1.00	80.00
				300.00

the table shows what price, quantity consumed and supplied, and buyers' expenditures would be without any intervention in the market. The second set of figures is constructed on the assumption that a buffer stock buys and sells as necessary to stabilize price. The remarkable fact is that the activities of the buffer stock reduce buyers' expenditures. Suppliers' revenues, of course, fall by the same amount.

This is not an accidental result that depends on the particular numerical values assumed. It is, instead, a general property of cases in which supply is stable while demand varies. It is not surprising that buyers would gain from price stabilization in these circumstances. At any given price, more is purchased when the level of demand is high than when it is low. For this reason alone, it seems likely that the gains from holding price down in a period of high demand exceed the costs to buyers when price is supported in a period of low demand.

The example in table 2-4 is intended only to establish that price stabilization has predictable effects on suppliers' revenues and buyers' expenditures. This line of argument is pursued in chapter 3. Drawing from results in the literature, it is shown there: (1) that, in a competitive market, there are net gains to reducing price fluctuations, in the sense that the *sum* of suppliers' and buyers' profits is increased; and (2) that the distribution of the gains, i.e., whether suppliers, or buyers, or both gain depends on the relative variability of supply and demand.

Stabilization Mechanisms

The discussion has so far identified the broad economic considerations that enter into debates on the proper role of commodity agreements. Put in terms of direct objectives, these are:

1. Maintenance of commodity prices above the long-run competitive level, which implies transfers of income to the LDCs.
2. Prevention of drastic declines in the LDCs' export earnings and/or commodity prices.
3. Reduction of fluctuations in commodity prices.

These objectives are not mutually exclusive, and therein lies one of the major complications in the debate on commodity agreements. The distinction between maintaining price above the competitive level and reducing price fluctuations is clear, but it is not clear what the distinction implies in organizational terms. To make further progress, then, it is necessary to identify the various types of stabilization mechanisms.

Methods of Market Intervention[17]

A useful start on this task can be made by noting that most commodity prices are established on terminal markets (organized exchanges). Quantities demanded and supplied are registered on an organized exchange, and the price established balances quantities offered for sale with what buyers are willing to purchase.[18]

An International Commodity Organization (ICO) can intervene in such a market in one of two broad ways: purchases and/or sales, and restrictions on supply (export quotas or production controls).[19] The possible types of commodity arrangements are:

1. Purchase alone, with the material acquired held in storage indefinitely or disposed of in a way that does not affect market price.
2. Purchases coupled with restrictions on supply.
3. Purchases and sales without any restrictions on supply.
4. Restrictions on supply alone.
5. Purchases and sales coupled with restrictions on supply.

There are, of course, many variations within each of these categories.

Domestic agricultural programs provide examples of the first two items on this list. These programs are usually geared to a support price, which the government stands ready to maintain by purchasing any excess supply. This requires purchases in good crop years and, to the extent that the support price is above the competitive price, more or less continuous purchases. The result is an ever-increasing stockpile, acquired at substantial cost, which leads to pressures for reducing supply. Some U.S. programs have attempted, without great success, to use voluntary limitations on supply agreed to through agricultural marketing boards. Soil bank and acreage allotment programs instead rely on payments to induce producers to limit their output. In effect, the government pays for a reduction in output rather than buying the surplus.

The third item on the list is a pure buffer stock. Buffer stocks are often confused with domestic agricultural programs, but they are quite different. A pure buffer stock involves no use at all of restrictions on supply. Furthermore, it would have only a fixed capital, and its rules would require both purchases and sales in appropriate circumstances.

Figure 2-1 illustrates the notion of a pure buffer stock. The upper panel describes the determination of price in the absence of a buffer stock for a simple case. The demand curve D is assumed to be stable. Long-run supply, $S(\overline{P})$, which can be interpreted as the number of acres planted times the average yield per acre, is assumed to depend on average price over several years ($\overline{P}$). Short-run supply is assumed to be independent of price and, given that planned or average

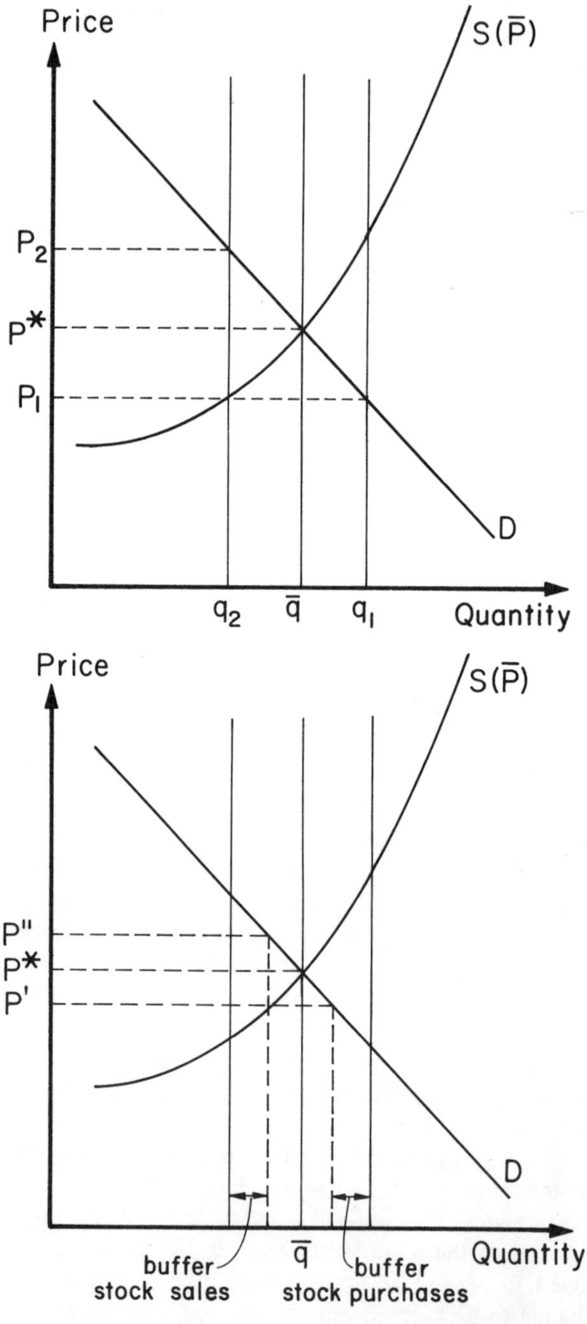

Figure 2-1. Operation of a Pure Buffer Stock

production is $\overline{q}$, short-run supply is assumed to vary randomly between q_1 (good crop years) and q_2 (bad crop years). For the assumptions built into figure 2-1, the long-run equilibrium price is P^*. In the short run, price varies from a high of P_2 in bad crop years, to P^* in average years to a low of P_1 in good crop years. The lower panel in the figure describes the operation of the buffer stock. The target price is P^*, and the floor and ceiling prices are denoted P' and P'', respectively. In good crop years, the buffer stock would make purchases equal to the difference between supply and demand at price P', and in bad crop years, the buffer stock would make sales equal to the difference between quantity demanded and supplied at price P''. For the simple case shown, purchases would be equal to sales. The average of the floor and ceiling price is the long-run equilibrium price P^*. (The operation of a pure buffer stock arrangement is by no means so simple and certain as these comments might suggest. A discussion of these complications, however, is postponed to the following chapter.)

Past international commodity agreements have largely relied on measures to control supply (item 4). In such arrangements, suppliers negotiate market shares and a floor price, and exports and/or production are then restricted as necessary to maintain the floor price. Within the United States, it is usually taken for granted that market sharing arrangements, or any other restrictions on supply, are anticompetitive and therefore undesirable. Discussions of international commodity agreements often assume instead that restrictions on supply can be used to limit price declines without raising price above the competitive level. There is no doubt, however, that unless unlimited funds for purchases are available, restrictions on supply are necessary if price is to be maintained above the competitive level.

Figure 2-2 provides a formal description of the role of reductions in supply in maintaining price above the long-run competitive level P^*. The upper panel shows the situation without intervention. It is assumed in the lower panel that the support price is $\tilde{P}$. At this price, quantity $\tilde{q}_d$ is demanded while, in the absence of restrictions, planned output would be the larger amount $\tilde{q}_s$. To maintain $\tilde{P}$, it is first necessary to limit planned production (or plantings or capacity) to $\tilde{q}_d$. This requires production controls and, since at any price above the long-run competitive level investment in the industry is attractive, limitations on entry and expansion by existing suppliers. Second, in good crop years, maintaining $\tilde{P}$ requires limiting shipments to $\tilde{q}_d$.

The ambiguities in the role of supply management carry over to the fifth of the arrangements, a buffer stock combined with restrictions on supply. It is possible to arrive at such a mixed arrangement from either of two directions. First, it can be argued that restrictions on supply should be available for use in emergency situations, such as a very sharp decline in demand caused by a recession in the DCs. Second, a buffer stock provides a convenient way of soaking up part of any excess supply created by a price above the competitive level. But whatever the rationale, there is a question as to whether a buffer stock

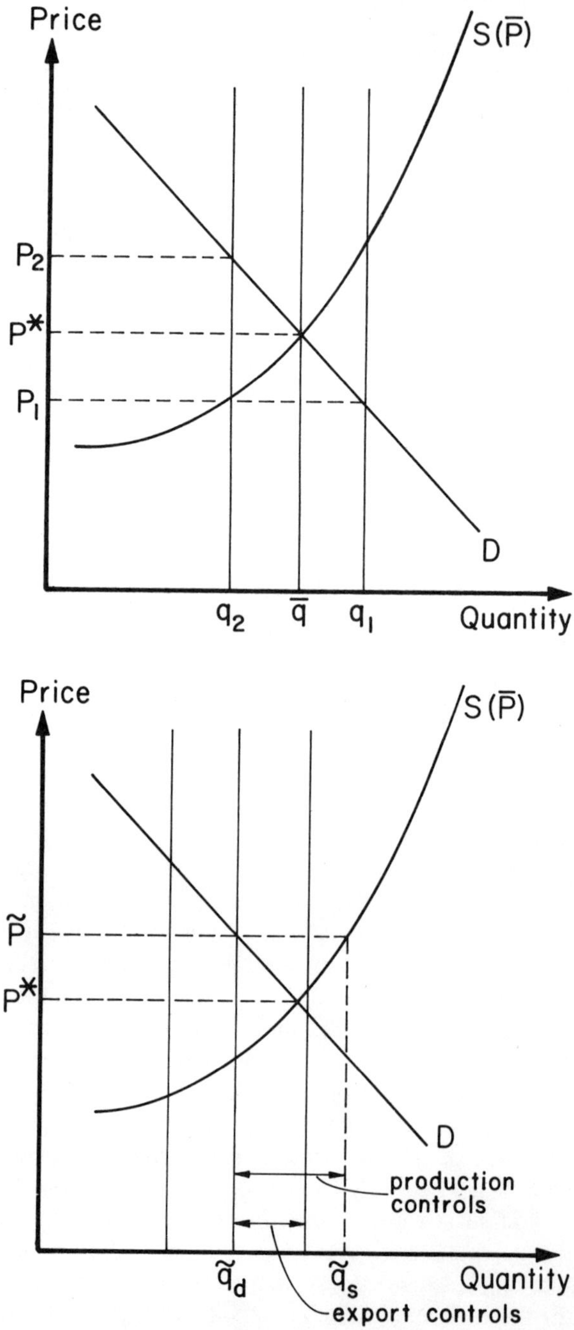

Figure 2-2. Operation of a Restrictive Commodity Agreement

with supply management would function as essentially a pure buffer stock or as a restrictive scheme.

Compensatory Financing

The stabilization of the LDCs' export earnings would not require intervention in the commodity markets. In fact, the direct approach to smoothing fluctuations is not controls on supplies or a buffer stock, which act only indirectly on export earnings, but transfers between exporting nations and an international agency. This is the idea behind compensatory financing. From an exporting nation's perspective, a compensatory financing arrangement would be much like a savings account. Withdrawals would be made in periods of below-average export earnings and deposits (or repayments) made in periods of above-average export earnings.

A compensatory financing scheme might be based on the total export earnings of member countries or on their export earnings from individual commodities. The principles would be much the same in either case, but it is convenient to think in terms of compensatory financing for total exports.

A compensatory financing arrangement would begin with a fixed capital contributed by importing and/or exporting nations, but instead of target price, its operations would be governed by a measure of the exporting nations' base export earnings. The bases might be specified in a variety of ways, but a moving average of past export earnings is an obvious choice. Whenever a country's export earnings fell below, say, 90 percent of its base, the compensatory financing facility would attempt to make up the shortfall.[20] If this were impossible, the funds available would be allocated in accord with some fixed formula (for example, in proportion to base export earnings or in proportion to initial contributions). Transfers made to countries during periods of below-average export earnings would eventually be repaid. It is in the spirit of the savings bank analogy to require that repayments be made whenever export earnings rise more than perhaps 10 percent above the base, but there are other possibilities.

Compensatory financing would not act to limit declines in commodity prices and production, which raises the question of the extent to which this scheme meets the crucial problems. The major agricultural exports of the LDCs are typically made through government marketing boards. These boards tend to insulate domestic producers but not the government from fluctuations in market price. In these cases, the problem is primarily one of export earnings and not of prices and production as such. The situation for the metals is somewhat different because production is often in the hands of the government, and metals production is, for several countries, a major source of both employment and export earnings. Compensatory financing would respond directly only to declines in export earnings, but it would provide the means for dealing with the problem of employment. Given that export earnings are maintained, the country could choose to maintain production and either sell the material or hold it in inventory. Or production could be cut and those laid off paid unemployment benefits. Compensatory financing, then, not only meets the problem but provides a significant degree of flexibility.

Compensatory financing for a single commodity is the financial analog of a pure buffer stock. In periods when the market is soft, the buffer stock would buy to support price and hence exporters' revenues. In a tight market, a buffer stock would sell to hold prices down, which would recover its capital and reduce exporters' earnings from what they would be otherwise. Compensatory financing for a single commodity would involve the same pattern of payment and repayment, but made directly rather than indirectly via price changes.

Objectives and Instruments

Table 2-5 lists the various stabilization measures and describes their direct and indirect effects on price and export earnings. These mechanisms fall roughly into a hierarchy in which successive arrangements take on additional roles. Compensatory financing would only reduce fluctuations in export earnings, and a pure buffer stock would reduce fluctuations in both export earnings and price. A buffer stock with supply management could reduce fluctuations in price and export earnings and maintain price above the long-run competitive level. The other mechanisms would also maintain price above the competitive level and limit declines in export earnings but, unlike a buffer stock, would not have any means of limiting price increases.

Each of the mechanisms shown in table 2-5 would limit declines in the LDCs' export earnings. Simple though it is, this is an important point. The proposition that periodic collapses in export earnings are an obstacle to development argues for the creation of some sort of stabilization arrangement, though not for any particular alternative. Choices among alternative mechanisms must be made on some other basis.

This problem is usually seen as one of matching mechanisms to the particular characteristics of individual commodities.[21] For example, storage costs vary from one commodity to the next as do the difficulties involved in enforcing controls on supply. Casting the issue in these terms, however, brushes aside the problem of matching mechanisms and objectives and so obscures the major differences of opinion on the proper objectives of commodity arguments.

This difference is reflected in the mechanisms that appear in table 2-5. Compensatory financing and pure buffer stocks do not involve transfers of real resources to the LDCs. Permanent controls on supply, and price supports, with or without controls on supply, would result in transfers to the LDCs. A buffer

Table 2-5
Direct and Indirect Effects of Stabilization Mechanisms

Mechanism	*Direct Effects on Price*	*Effects on Export Earnings*	*Transfers of Income to Suppliers*
1. Compensatory financing	None	Reduce fluctuations in export earnings	No
2. Pure buffer stock	Reduce price fluctuations	Reduce fluctations in export earnings	No
3. Buffer stock with controls on supply	Reduce price fluctuations and possibly maintain price above the long-run competitive level	Reduce fluctuations in export earnings and possibly increase average export earnings	Uncertain
4. Price supports with permanent controls on supply	Limit price declines and maintain price above the long-run competitive level	Limit declines in export earnings and increase average export earnings	Yes
5. Permanent controls on supply	Limit price declines and maintain price above the long-run competitive level	Limit declines in export earnings and increase average export earnings	Yes
6. Price supports	Limit price declines and maintain price above the long-run competitive level	Limit declines in export earnings and increase average export earnings	Yes

stock with provisions for supply management might result in significant transfers depending on how controls on supply are employed. The choice of means within each of these two groups is properly based on cost (that is, given the objective, the least costly means should be used. It should be added that cost here does not simply mean expenditures by governments or an international agency but includes all costs, private and public, associated with a commodity arrangement.)

Income Transfers

Transfers of income made via higher prices are one of the ways in which commodity agreements might be used to speed the LDCs' development. There is a question (pursued in chapters 4 and 5) about the feasibility of using commodity arrangements to maintain prices above the competitive level, but there is a prior question as to whether, compared to the alternatives, price increases are an appropriate way to make transfers.

Price increases cost donors (buyers) more than recipients (suppliers) receive and set up secondary distortions in the use of resources, which tend to reduce the total value of goods and services available.[22] Direct transfers, which, with some qualifications means development assistance programs, cost donors only the amount of the transfer. Considering both public and private costs, then, any transfer can be made at lower cost directly than via price increases.

In view of the inefficiency of making transfers by price increases, any case for doing so must rest on political considerations. Price increases might be the only politically feasible way to make transfers, or, by agreeing to help maintain prices above the competitive level, the DCs might avoid some political costs and/or obtain political advantages.

These possibilities are not necessarily compelling. If, nevertheless, commodity agreements are to be used to increase prices, the choice of means is between purchases, which implies a continual accumulation of stocks, and restrictions on supply. Restrictions on supply require no governmental expenditures but impose costs on buyers via higher prices, while purchases both impose costs on buyers and require expenditures by governments. Thus, considering both governmental and private costs, it is cheaper to transfer a given amount of revenue through controls on supply than by purchases. Although the argument cannot be made so simply, this is correct if demand is inelastic.[23]

In a smoothly functioning restrictive arrangement, capacity would be adjusted to average demand at the desired price. Controls on supply would be used to limit declines in price, but large increases in price could not be prevented. If a floor price would be maintained in any event, addition of a buffer stock would tend to benefit buyers because it would to some degree limit price increases. A buffer stock might also ameliorate the problems that tend to affect restrictive arrangements, but if the purpose of an arrangement is to maintain price above the competitive level, a buffer stock has no crucial role to play. Given that continual purchases are ruled out, controls on supply are the key to maintaining price about the competitive level.

Fluctuations in Price and Export Earnings

The use of commodity agreements to transfer income is a relatively simple case. The problems are more complex if commodity agreements are rejected as a means of making price increases but accepted as a way of reducing fluctuations in prices and export earnings. This position presents a choice among instruments and involves aspects of both economic development and the mutual advantage of buyers and sellers.

Buffer stocks are not feasible for all commodities, and the supply of many commodities would be very difficult to control. In contrast, compensatory financing is a very flexible mechanism. For that reason, it is useful to assume that a compensatory financing arrangement is in existence and ask what reasons there are to substitute a buffer stocks or controls on supply. It is also useful to suppose that, whatever mechanism is used, declines in the LDCs' export earnings would be limited to the same extent. The question of whether there is a case for substituting a buffer stock or controls on supply for compensatory financing can then be approached on a commodity-by-commodity basis.

Table 2-6 is a brief summary of the immediate effects on price, output, revenue, and so forth of compensatory financing, pure buffer stocks, and controls on supply. It is assumed that compensatory financing would require full repayment but that no interest would be charged on transfers. The entries for a pure buffer stock reflect conclusions stated above and developed more fully in chapter 3. Finally, the entries for controls on supply state the fact that suppliers gain less from restrictions on supply than buyers lose.

Compensatory financing and a buffer stock require a repayment of transfers; exporting nations would presumably contribute to capital costs in both cases. Supply management measures would not involve any capital costs and would limit declines in price and export earnings without choking off increases. It is clear, then, that producers' gains under supply management exceed those under a buffer stock or compensatory financing. Suppliers would rank a buffer stock second in those cases where they gain directly from the reduction of price fluctuations and third otherwise.

Buyers' ranking in terms of direct economic effects would be the reverse. So long as demand is not perfectly inelastic, the costs to buyers of controls on supply exceed the transfer to suppliers. Since the disbursements made by a compensatory financing arrangement would equal the transfer to suppliers, this implies that a transfer can be made more cheaply via compensatory financing than by controls on supply. A buffer stock would sometimes support price and

Table 2-6
Major Direct Effects, Except Capital Costs, on Buyers and Suppliers of Compensatory Financing, Buffer Stocks, and Controls on Supply

	Direct Benefits and Costs to Suppliers			*Direct Benefits and Costs to Buyers*			*Net Direct Benefits to Suppliers and Buyers*
Mechanism	*Benefits*	*Costs*	*Net Benefits*	*Benefits*	*Costs*	*Net Benefits*	
Compensatory financing	Transfer when export earnings are below average	Repayment when export earnings are above average	0	0	0	0	0
Pure buffer stock	Increased revenue when purchases are made to support price	Reduced revenue when sales are made to reduce price	±	Lower price when sales are made	Higher price when purchases are made	±	+
Controls on supply	Increased revenue and profit when supply is restricted	0	+	0	Higher price when supply is restricted	–	–

sometimes hold price down, while controls on supply would only support price. For this reason, there is a presumption that buyers would be better off with a buffer stock than with controls on supply.[24] Buyers, then, would consider both compensatory financing and a buffer stock as more desirable than controls on supply.

The implications that are attached to the conflicting rankings of buyers and sellers depend on what sort of arrangements are regarded as possible. Under ideal circumstances, clashes of this sort can be resolved by adopting the alternative that provides the largest net benefits, without regard to distribution, and then working out a satisfactory distribution of net benefits. Finding a satisfactory distribution can be very difficult, but within the context of a related set of commodity arrangements, the possibility would seem to be of more than theoretical interest. If this is granted, the appropriate criterion for choice among alternative mechanisms is the sum of net benefits to buyers and sellers.

Controls on supply obviously rank last on this criterion. The question is the ranking of compensatory financing and buffer stocks. Compensatory financing would not have systematic effects on commodity prices, and a buffer stock would act directly to reduce fluctuations in commodity prices and indirectly to reduce fluctuations in the LDCs' export earnings. There are net gains to reducing price fluctuations, but sellers could gain while buyers could lose, or buyers could gain while sellers lose. These facts pose a problem in sharing the costs of a buffer stock, but, if this problem can be resolved, the fact there are net gains to price stabilization is an argument for the use of buffer stocks.

Capital costs are a second consideration. Buffer stock purchases benefit suppliers both by maintaining price above what it would otherwise be and by increasing suppliers' sales. This points to the possibility that the transfer achieved by a buffer stock could exceed its expenditures, which proves to be the case. Appendix A to this book presents a computation of the ratio of increased revenues created by buffer stock purchases to the buffer stock's expenditures for a simple model, which assumes that shifts in each of supply and demand alone are sufficient to change output from its base level by 10 percent and that a buffer stock trades to maintain price within ±10 percent of the target price. The results obtained are shown in the first column of table 2-7. In each case, the increase in suppliers' revenues is at least as large as computed buffer stock expenditures; for most of the commodities, it is substantially larger.

There are, however, two offsetting factors. First, a buffer stock would incur storage costs. It might, however, also earn a trading profit, and the available evidence suggests that this would be sufficient to offset storage costs. Second, not all of the increase in revenues would go to suppliers in the LDCs. The third column of table 2-7 presents rough estimates, constructed using the fraction of the commodity exported by LDCs, of the ratio of LDCs' increased revenues to buffer stock expenditures. For all but three of these commodities, this ratio exceeds unity, implying that the capital costs of supporting the LDCs' export

Table 2-7
Ratio of Increases in Revenue to Suppliers to Buffer Stock Expenditures for a Simple Model

Commodity	*Ratio of Increased Revenue to Buffer Stock Expenditures*	*Percent of Commodity Exported by LDCs*	*Ratio of Increased Revenue to LDCs to Buffer Stock Expenditures*
Cocoa	1.2	99.2	1.19
Coffee	1.3	96.8	1.23
Tea	1.6	82.8	1.32
Cotton	1.2	57.9	0.69
Sugar	1.6	69.7	1.12
Jute	1.6	95.6	1.53
Sisal	1.0	97.7	0.98
Rubber	1.4	97.7	1.37
Copper	1.5	54.5	0.82
Tin	2.0	85.5	1.70

Sources: Appendix to this book and International Bank for Reconstruction and Development, *Commodity Trade and Price Trends* (1975).

earnings by a buffer stock are less than those of compensatory financing. The exceptions are cotton, copper, and sisal. In these cases, a buffer stock has a cost disadvantage, although this might be offset by the benefits to reducing price fluctuations.

The existence of direct gains to buyers and/or sellers from reducing price fluctuations implies that buffer stocks for some commodities might be warranted by a cost/benefit analysis done without regard to the effects on instability of export earnings on development. This discussion, however, is concerned with the use of buffer stocks as a substitute for compensatory financing, which, in turn, would find its justification in the effects of instability in export earnings on the LDCs. A reduction in fluctuations in export earnings could, for most cases, be obtained at lower cost with a buffer stock. Even when a buffer stock is the more expensive alternative, the gains to reducing price fluctuations might be sufficient to overcome the cost disadvantage of a buffer stock. In summary, then, there is an economic case for some use of buffer stocks in place of compensatory financing.

Buffer Stocks with Supply Management

The arrangements usually proposed are not pure buffer stocks but buffer stocks with provisions for the use of supply management. It is taken for granted that there is a need for supply management as a supplemental or supporting measure. But controls on supply can also be used to hold prices above the competitive level, and if an ICO has recourse to supply management, the line between reducing price fluctuations and increasing the average level of prices would be very difficult to maintain. There is good reason, then, to look very carefully at the question of whether controls on supply have a legitimate role to play in a buffer stock arrangement.

The use of supply management alters the distribution and the magnitude of the gains to a buffer stock arrangement. Suppose that controls on supply are used to reduce buffer stock purchases and that the substitution is made so that suppliers' revenues in periods when price is supported are the same as they would be under purchases. The results obtained in appendix A to this book imply that price must then be supported at a higher level to maintain suppliers' revenues or profits at some fixed amount. Although these comments ignore capital costs and so are not conclusive, they suggest that the use of controls on supply increases gains to suppliers, reduces gains to buyers, and reduces net benefits.

The arguments usually offered for the use of supply management, however, proceed from the limitations of a buffer stock rather than from distributional considerations. A pure buffer stock could not guarantee that the floor price would be maintained. In particular, a buffer stock with some given capital might be able to cope with the effects of a recession that went on for, say, seven quarters, but not longer. Against this possibility, it is argued that the inclusion of supply management measures provides greater certainty that the floor price can be defended.

While this is so, it is not clear why greater certainty is required or why controls on supply are the appropriate response. These questions should be viewed against the idea of a buffer stock of optimal scale. The benefits of a buffer stock lie in the reductions in fluctuations in price and the LDCs' export earnings. As the size of a buffer stock (measured by its capital) increases, benefits increase, but so do costs; the buffer stock is at an optimal scale when the expected benefits from an increase in scale are exactly offset by the additional costs. The question to ask then is: Given that the scale of the buffer stock is optimal, what is the reason for controls on supply?

The answer can lie only in costs. It has already been noted that controls on supply are generally the most expensive of the alternatives when both public and private costs are considered. However, the prospect of a severe, prolonged recession does pose a question of cost or, better, feasibility.

Estimates presented in the following chapter indicate that the combination of a recession and a good crop year could require a buffer stock to acquire a four to six months' supply to defend a floor price 10 percent below the target price. A recession that persisted for three years could easily require purchases of a year to eighteen months' supply to defend the floor price. If the recession were followed by a mild recovery and slow growth, several years might elapse before there was a call for significant sales in defense of the ceiling price. To the extent that purchases made during the recession must be held for a long period, the buffer stock becomes more like a price support program and less like an organization that trades to reduce price fluctuations. This problem raises the question of whether there is a less costly means than purchases.

The choice is between compensatory financing and controls on supply. It is sometimes argued that buyers benefit indirectly from controls on supply. The reasoning behind this proposition rests on the assertion that recessions lead to declines in capacity. If so, recoveries produce periods of high prices, which could be partially avoided by maintaining capacity in place. Severe recessions can force suppliers from the market, but there is no evidence that postwar recessions have in fact produced significant declines in capacity in the commodity industries, and there is a presumption that they have not. First, postwar recessions have been relatively brief and mild. Second, in most of the commodity industries, capacity is only very slowly adjusted to declines in price. Consequently, the proposition that buyers would indirectly benefit from controls on supply seems insubstantial, and the particular circumstances considered here do not alter the earlier conclusion that compensatory financing is cheaper than controls on supply. Hence, insofar as problems created by the business cycle are concerned, the appropriate supplemental measure is compensatory financing.

A second and entirely different argument for the inclusion of supply management measures starts from the correct assumption that a pure buffer stock could not deal with permanent adjustments in the market. If a buffer stock is to maintain its ability to reduce price fluctuations, it must stand aside when permanent adjustments in the market occur. For example, a pure buffer stock would not attempt to limit a decline in price because of a permanent decline in demand.

The variable cost of producing some agricultural commodities is very low, and these commodities are often grown by small landowners who cannot readily shift to other crops or occupations. In these circumstances, price can remain very low for many years before producers leave the market. This raises humanitarian issues and may also involve an inefficient use of resources.

Cutbacks in the outputs of all suppliers, however, would not speed the adjustment process. On the contrary, to the extent that restriction of supply increases the revenues of all suppliers, the adjustment process would be slowed down and perhaps stopped. Hence, if restrictions on supply have any role at all to play, they must be used to reduce the number of producers in the market. Those so removed would not be helped by such restrictions. Presumably, then, any use of restrictions on supply to decrease the number of suppliers should be coupled with programs to ease the burden of transition and investments for diversification (that is, the creation of new employment opportunities).

Once this step is taken, it is necessary to ask why production controls are needed at all. By hypothesis, the producers are in extremely difficult straits, and the diversification program would offer them better opportunities. It may be that administrative and/or sociological factors provide an answer to this question, but it is clear that the burden shifts to diversification programs and away from export controls.

Altogether the case for the use of supply management in conjunction with a buffer stock is virtually nonexistent. At most, there is a case for the use of supply restrictions at the national level as a subordinate part of a diversification program. This conclusion assumes that the purpose of the arrangement is simply to reduce fluctuations in price and/or the LDCs' export earnings. If the purpose is also to maintain price above the competitive level, restrictions on supply clearly have a vital role to play.

Concluding Comments

This discussion yields three conclusions and a dilemma. The first conclusion is that controls on supply are the appropriate means if the objective is to maintain price above the competitive level. Second, there is an economic case for some use of buffer stocks in place of compensatory financing, given that a case has been made for reducing fluctuations in the LDCs' export earnings. Third, there is no role for controls on supply if the purpose of a buffer stock arrangement is only to reduce price fluctuations.

The dilemma is the ambiguous character of a buffer stock with supply management, an all-purpose instrument in the sense that it could be used to reduce price fluctuations, prevent large declines in price, and maintain price above the competitive level. It is not to the point, then, to debate whether a buffer stock would simply reduce price fluctuations or would also maintain price above the competitive level. The distinction between these two possibilities does not lie with the buffer stock itself but with the use that is made of controls on supply. There are two polar cases: a pure buffer stock, (a buffer stock that makes no use of supply management) and an arrangement that does not include a buffer stock but employs restrictions on supply in an attempt to maintain price above the competitive level.

Notes

1. The coefficient of variation is the ratio of the standard deviation of a series to its average. For example, if the values in the series are independently and normally distributed, a value of 0.1 for the coefficient of variation means that values will be within ±10 percent of the mean value about two-thirds of the time.

2. Guy F. Erb and Salvatore Shiavo-Campo, "Economic Instability, Level of Development, and Economic Size of Less Developed Countries," *Bulletin of the Oxford University Institute of Economics and Statistics* 31 (1969):263-283.

3. This is essentially the position taken by Odin Knudsen and Andrew Parnes, *Trade Instability and Economic Development* (Lexington, Mass.: Lexington Books, 1975), Cf. pp. 23-25.

4. See Joseph D. Coppock, *International Economic Instability* (New York: McGraw-Hill, 1962), Michael Michaely, *Concentration in International Trade* (Amsterdam: North-Holland Publishing Co., 1962), Alasdair I. McBean, *Export Instability and Economic Development* (Cambridge: Harvard University Press, 1966), and for a brief review of the literature on the causes of instability in export earnings, Knudsen and Parnes, *Trade Instability*, chap. 2.

5. See Statement of Raúl Prebish, Secretary-General of UNCTAD, in UNCTAD, *Trade and Development: Commodity Trade*, E/CONF. 46/141 (New York: United Nations, 1964), pp. 76-81; see also the remarks by Prebish in John Carey, ed., *Law and Policy-Making for Trade Among "Have" and "Have-Not" Nations* (Dobbs Ferry, N.Y.: Oceana Publication, Inc., for the Association of the Bar of the City of New York, 1968), pp. 52-60.

6. See Harry G. Johnson, *Economic Policies Towards Less Developed Countries* (Washington, D.C.: The Brookings Institution, 1967), and Vernon L. Sorenson, *International Trade Policy: Agriculture and Development* (East Lansing: Division of Research, Graduate School of Business Administration, Michigan State University, 1975).

7. Statement of the secretary-general of UNCTAD (Gamani Corea) at the opening meeting of the first preparatory conference for negotiations on a Common Fund; in UNCTAD, "Report of the First Preparatory Meeting for the Negotiation of a Common Fund," TD/B/IPC/CF/4, December 22, 1976.

8. See McBean, *Export Instability*, chap. 1, for a summary of these arguments.

9. Ibid.

10. Knudsen and Parnes, *Trade Instability*.

11. A. Maizels, "Review of Export Instability and Economic Growth," *American Economic Review* 58 (June 1968):575-580.

12. B.F. Massell, S.R. Pearson, and J.B. Fitch, "Foreign Exchange and Economic Development: An Empirical Study of Selected Latin American Countries," *Review of Economics and Statistics* 54 (1972):208-212.

13. C. Rangarajan and V. Sundararajan, "Impact of Export Fluctuations on Income–A Cross-Country Analysis," *Review of Economics and Statistics* 58 (August 1976):368-372.

14. In particular, the fact that prices are not so sticky as they seem to be. See G. Stigler and J. Kendahl, *The Behavior of Industrial Prices* (New York: National Bureau of Economic Research, 1970).

15. *Economic Report of the President 1977* (Washington, D.C.: Government Printing Office, 1977), pp. 198, 299.

16. Charles River Associates, *Public and Private Stockpiling for Future Shortages,* Report to the National Commission on Supplies and Shortages, August 1976, provides an analytical treatment of this issue.

17. Much more detailed discussions of stabilization mechanisms can be found in J.W.F. Rowe, *Primary Commodities in International Trade* (Cambridge: Cambridge University Press, 1965), chap. 14, and Commodities Research Unit, Ltd., *Co-ordinated National Stockpiles as a Market Stabilizing Mechanism–Copper* (London and New York: Commodities Research Unit, Ltd., 1977).

18. Orders to buy or sell usually must be placed with authorized traders. Although the details of the process vary from one exchange to another, it is typical for traders to gather in a "pit" (usually a platform) in which the commodity is traded and shout out the price at which they are currently willing to buy or sell. If demand exceeds supply, it quickly becomes apparent that buyers must increase their bids. Conversely, if the quantity offered exceeds that demanded, bids and closing prices fall.

19. A commodity sold on an organized exchange cannot be rationed, in the usual sense of that term, as price adjusts to equate available supplies with quantity demanded. Two price systems are possible, however. For a discussion of two price systems in the copper industry, see David McNicol, "The Two Price Systems in the Copper Industry," *Bell Journal of Economics* 6 (Spring 1975):50-73.

20. The International Monetary Fund's small compensatory financing facility also involves a balance-of-payment test.

21. This approach is taken in UNCTAD documents on the integrated program. See especially UNCTAD, *Trade and Development: Final Act and Report,* E/CONF. 46/141, vol. 1 (New York: United Nations, 1964), pp. 1-67, and UNCTAD, "An Integrated Programme for Commodities: Measures for Individual Commodities," report by the UNCTAD Secretariat, TD/B/C.1/194, October 1, 1975.

22. If demand is completely inelastic, the buyers' loss is equal to the suppliers' gain. But if demand is to some degree responsive to price, buyers lose both by the higher price caused by controls and by the induced fall in demand. The formal development of this point can be found in any introductory economics text under the heading "deadweight loss to monopoly."

23. The result obtained in appendix A to this book implies that price is lower if a transfer of a given size is made by purchases rather than controls. Cost to buyers is then lower if purchases are used. However, it can be shown that the sum of purchase costs and the costs to buyers because of higher prices is, for a given transfer, higher if the transfer is made by purchase. Proof of this point is omitted since the conclusion that restriction of supply is superior to purchases as a means of maintaining price above the competitive level is not disputed.

24. It can be easily shown, for the simple cases discussed in chapter 3, that if capital costs are ignored, the use of controls on supply reduces the direct benefits to buyers and increases the direct benefits to suppliers of reducing price fluctuations. However, the analysis becomes much more complex when capital costs are considered.

3 Pure Buffer Stock Arrangements

Nations maintain stocks for various reasons. The classic example is agricultural stocks held against the possibility of crop failures; more modern examples are stocks of strategic materials held by the United States and other nations. Price support programs are also a familiar feature of economic life in both the DCs and the LDCs. Buffer stocks, however, are neither contingency stocks nor price support arrangements. A buffer stock is intended to maintain prices when the market is soft and to hold price down in a tight market. There has been very little experience with buffer stock arrangements. In terms of history, the idea of a pure buffer stock (which involves no restrictions on supply) is a new one that should be evaluated on its merits.

Character of a Pure Buffer Stock

A buffer stock would be in the hands of an International Commodity Organization (ICO) created by a commodity agreement. The ICO would hold title to the stocks purchased and the funds involved in the operation of the buffer stock, and its professional staff would be responsible for the conduct of trading. Within the limits set by the agreement, policy would be made by a governing council composed of representatives of the agreement's member nations.

A pure buffer stock arrangement would begin with a fixed capital, contributed by member nations, which could be augmented by borrowing. The trading rules of a buffer stock would probably be specified in terms of a target price and floor and ceiling prices set at some percentage (such as ±10 percent) of the target price. Sales would be made to defend the ceiling price, and, subject to some exceptions, the buffer stock would be required to buy to defend the floor price. By definition, a pure buffer stock arrangement would not involve any restrictions on supply; it would buy and sell but would not regulate the activities of other traders.

Figure 3-1 shows estimates of the effects on price that a pure buffer stock for copper would have had over the years 1955-1973. The buffer stock would have supported the price of copper through the early 1960s and, by selling, would have avoided the high prices that prevailed during the 1965-1970 period and again in 1973.

Two aspects of these estimates are worth noting. First, the hypothetical

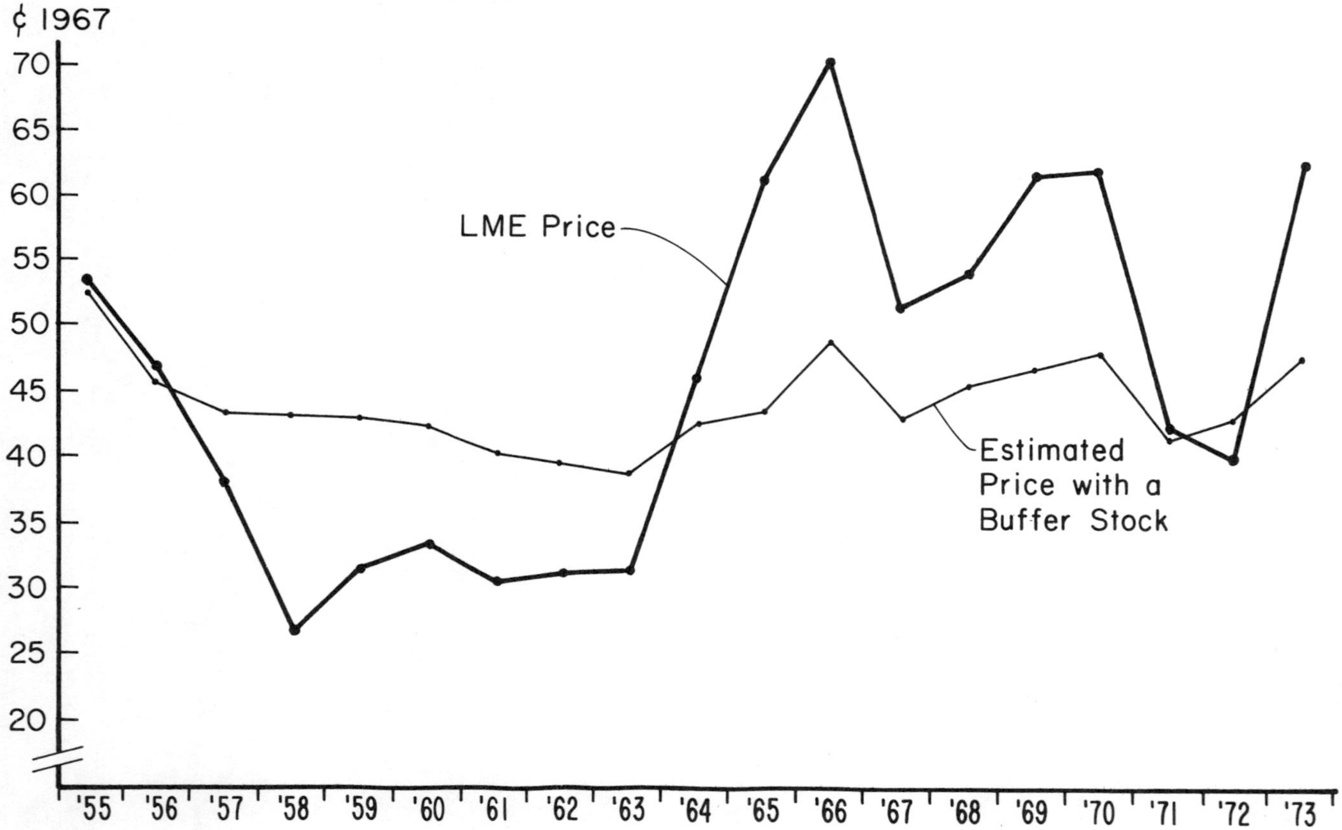

Source: U.S. Treasury, Office of Raw Material and Oceans Policy, *U.S. Commodity Policy* (February 1976).

Figure 3-1. Estimated Effects of a Buffer Stock on the London Metal Exchange Price of Copper, 1955-1973

buffer stock in copper was assumed to follow mechanical trading rules based on current and past prices. These assumed rules did not involve any forecasting, which is appropriate. A buffer stock manager would not be expected to do a better job of forecasting price movements than the market. On the contrary, a buffer stock should be understood as a form of insurance against unforeseen price changes. Second, the hypothetical copper buffer stock would not have altered the trend in copper prices over the simulation period, which, again, reflects a basic characteristic of a pure buffer stock. A pure buffer stock is intended only to (partially) filter out transitory changes in price. Changes in the weather are the principal source of transitory changes in agricultural prices, and swings in demand associated with the business cycle can also be counted as transitory changes, although they take place over a period of several years. The causes of permanent (or long-run) adjustments in a market can usually be reduced to changes in technology, a shift in consumer preferences, or the development of new resources. A pure buffer stock should accommodate itself to long-run adjustments rather than attempt to override them.

These comments provide a brief characterization of how a pure buffer stock arrangement should function. Whether it would in fact serve only to reduce price fluctuations, which is a major issue, is discussed in this and later chapters. If it is tentatively assumed that a buffer stock could be limited to the task of reducing price fluctuations, the question is whether doing so is worth the costs of the operation.

Costs and Benefits of Buffer Stocks

The capital costs and operating costs of a buffer stock would be met by governments, and the direct benefits would be received by buyers of the commodity and suppliers, which for some commodities are governments. Similar statements can be made about investments in highways, dams, schools, and so forth. In these cases, governments undertake investments to provide services that are not supplied by the market at all or are not supplied at an efficient level. Buffer stocks should be viewed in the same terms; for purposes of economic evaluation, they are a type of governmental investment project.

This section examines the benefits and costs of buffer stocks. While the results fall somewhat short of a full blown cost/benefit analysis, they provide a preliminary indication of the magnitude of the direct benefits of reducing price fluctuations and the costs of buffer stocks.

Costs of Buffer Stocks

Discussions of commodity agreements often seem to assume that the capital costs of establishing and operating a buffer stock would be modest. This assumption probably reflects the fact that the tin buffer stock—which is the only one to operate in the postwar years—is relatively inexpensive. But the International Tin Council buffer stock had a maximum size of 23,000 tons, which was too small to have much effect on tin prices.[1]

Capital Costs. The size of the stock that an ICO must be prepared to acquire depends on the magnitudes of shifts in supply and demand, the elasticities of supply and demand, and the degree of price stability that is desired. To take a simple case, suppose that the supply and demand curves are linear. Let f be the fraction by which price is permitted to decline from the target price. Denote base production by $\bar{q}$ and by z^*, the maximum amount that the buffer stock must acquire to defend the floor price. Finally, let $\nu^* \equiv z^*/\bar{q}$ be maximum buffer stock purchases as a fraction of base production. It is shown in appendix A that:

$$\nu^* = \frac{ag + \alpha h}{\bar{q}} - (\eta_s - \eta_d)f, \tag{3.1}$$

where a and α are, respectively, the intercepts of the demand and supply curves, g is the fraction by which demand shifts down in recession years, h is the fraction by which supply shifts out in good crop years, and η_s and η_d are, respectively, the elasticities of supply and demand. For values characteristic of the coffee industry:

$$\nu^* = 1.27 * g + 0.67 * h - 0.60 * f. \tag{3.2}$$

Figure 3-2 presents graphs of this relationship for alternative values of g and h. If demand is stable ($g = 0$) and supply varies by ±10 percent ($h = 0.1$), a buffer stock equal to only 0.7 percent of base output would, in this example, be sufficient to maintain price within ±10 percent of target ($f = 0.1$). However, for $g = 0.1$ and $h = 0.1$, the buffer stock must be prepared to acquire 13.4 percent of base production to maintain price within ±10 percent of target, and for $g = 0.1$ and $h = 0.2$, this value goes up to 20.1 percent of base production.

Table 3-1 presents estimates prepared by the UNCTAD Secretariat of the size of buffer stocks for the ten core commodities of the Integrated Programme. These results were computed using small econometric models. It was assumed that demand for each commodity would grow steadily and quite rapidly for the 1979-1983 period but that supply would be subject to random variations. A large number of alternative futures were generated by random drawings from the distributions of supply. The buffer stock sizes computed are those required to maintain price within ±10 percent of target price in 95 percent of these cases. It should be added that the UNCTAD report states that these estimates are of only indicative value.

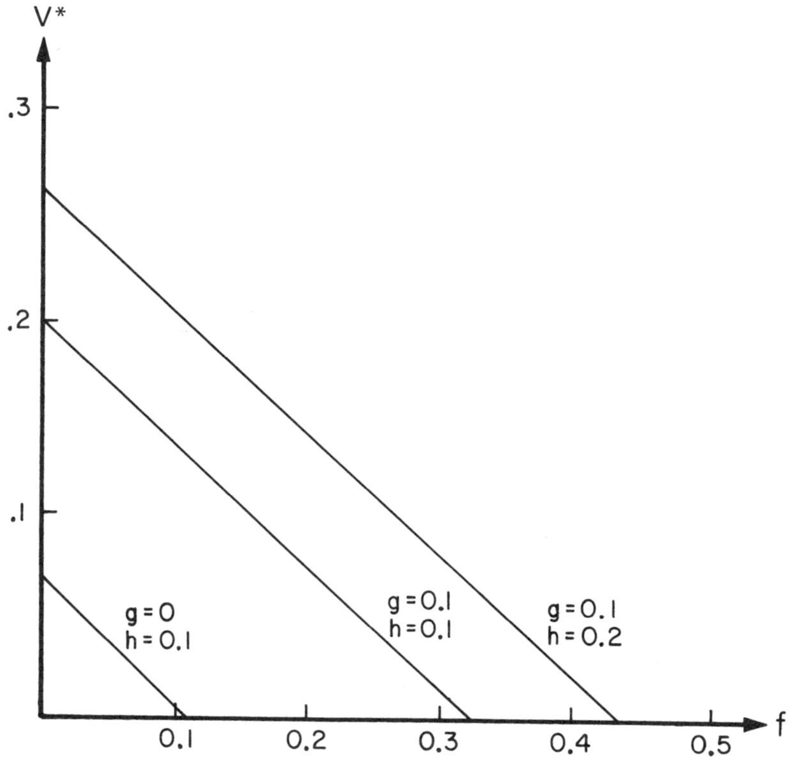

Figure 3-2. Variation of Maximum Buffer Stock Size, as a Fraction of Base Production, with the Degree of Price Instability

Studies of copper and tin buffer stocks done for the U.S. Treasury resulted in much larger estimates of capital requirements than the values given in table 3-1. These studies were based on econometric models of the copper and the tin industries, which were, with a hypothetical buffer stock incorporated in the model, simulated for the 1955-1973 period. The maximum size of the hypothetical copper buffer stock behind figure 3-1 was estimated to be 4.8 million tons, with an acquisition cost of roughly $5 billion.[2] It was estimated that a buffer stock capable of holding the London price of tin within ±10 percent of a five-year moving average of past prices from 1955 to 1973 would have had a maximum size of 385,000 tons with an acquisition cost of $900 million.[3]

The difference between these and the UNCTAD estimates must be largely explained by differing assumptions on demand. The UNCTAD Secretariat study assumes that industrial production in the Western nations will grow steadily and quite rapidly over the years 1979 to 1983; the period considered in the Treasury

Table 3-1
UNCTAD Secretariat Estimates of Stocks Sufficient to Maintain Price within ±10 Percent of Target, 1979-1983

Commodity	*Stock Requirements (1,000 tons)*	*Capital Requirements (1976 $ million)*
Cocoa	459	768
Coffee	680	1256
Tea	111	143
Sugar	4734	1934
Cotton	495	672
Jute[a]	420	174
Sisal[a]	149	86
Rubber	753	586
Copper	854	1365
Tin	37	267
Total		7,251[b]

Source: United Nations Conference on Trade and Development, *Common Fund: Financial Requirements*; note by the UNCTAD Secretariat; TD/B/IPC/CF/L.2, December 29, 1976, table 3, pp. 13-14.

Note: See text for a more detailed statement of the character of the estimates.

[a]Fiber only.

[b]Without pooling.

study (1955-1973) contained several recession years, and, in the face of a recession, larger stocks must be purchased and stocks acquired must be held for a longer period. Since recessions can be expected to occur from time to time, the U.S. Treasury study provides the more reliable estimates of capital costs for buffer stocks for copper and tin. The use of these values in place of those in table 3-1 would increase estimates of the total capital requirements of buffer stocks for the ten commodities from $7.3 billion to approximately $11.5 billion, and if the effects of the business cycle were systematically considered, the total presumably would be still larger.

The capital requirements of a buffer stock and its capital costs are not the same thing. A buffer stock would sometimes have its funds fully invested in the commodity; at other times, the capital of the buffer stock could be held in interest-bearing liquid assets. Suppose that these assets return 6 percent, that the opportunity cost of the buffer stock's capital is 15 percent, and that the buffer stock is fully committed two-thirds of the time. The annual average capital costs would be 8 percent (2/3 * 15% – 1/3 * 6%) of capital requirements.

The discussion so far has been of the capital costs of individual buffer stocks. Capital requirements, and hence capital costs, would be lower if a set of buffer stocks was operated jointly. Suppose, for example, that buffer stocks are to be operated for commodities A and B and that if these buffer stocks were operated independently, each would require a capital of $250 million. Assume further that the two markets are always exactly out of phase so that when buffer stock A is buying, buffer stock B is selling (and vice versa). The two buffer stocks could then be operated jointly with $250 million. If the two markets were exactly in phase with one another, then joint operation would still require $500 million. In general, to the extent that movements in the two markets are not perfectly correlated, the capital required to operate the two stocks together is less than $500 million.

The reduction in capital requirements does not itself measure the reduction in capital costs. If, again, it is assumed that markets A and B are invariably exactly out of phase with one another, buffer stock A would have $250 million invested in stocks of commodity A, when buffer stock B had its funds in cash, which could be invested in financial instruments. Looking at the two independently managed stocks together, only $250 million would be invested in the commodity at any one time. This is the amount that would be continuously invested in one or the other of the commodities if the two buffer stocks were managed jointly. Hence, if the individual stocks could make financial investments that paid exactly the opportunity cost of the funds that they employ, there would be no net gain to pooling.[4] However, a buffer stock would have to hold its funds in very liquid, low-risk assets, which would presumably return less than the opportunity cost of the buffer stock's capital. Pooling, then, could be expected to reduce capital costs by an amount equal to the reduction in funds required times the spread between the opportunity costs of the funds employed and the rate of return on safe, highly liquid assets.

Table 3-2 presents correlation coefficients for series on the deflated values of prices for thirteen commodities.[5] Of the seventy-eight values in the table, thirty-eight are either negative or zero, and most of the positive values are fairly small. It seems, then, that there is a good case for pooling. The UNCTAD Secretariat study mentioned above bears out this impression. Under each of four alternative sets of assumptions explored, pooling reduced the capital required by about 25 percent.[6] Again, however, the failure of the UNCTAD study to consider variations in demand to some extent vitiates its conclusions.

Other Costs. In addition to capital costs, the operation of a buffer stock would involve administrative costs, handling and storage costs, and a trading profit or loss (that is, the margin between receipts from sales of the stock and expenditures for its acquisition).

Table 3-3 provides some information on handling and storage costs for the ten core commodities. The first two columns present estimates of handling and annual storage costs. Given these values, the figures in the third column are the cost of moving the maximum stock (from table 3-1) into warehouses, storing it

Table 3-2
Correlations among Deflated Commodity Prices

Commodity	*Cocoa*	*Coffee*	*Tea*	*Sugar*	*Cotton*	*Jute*	*Sisal*	*Rubber*	*Copper*	*Tin*	*Wheat*	*Rice*
Coffee	0.08											
Tea	–.28	0.43										
Sugar	.33	–.24	–0.47									
Cotton	.30	.38	.19	0.06								
Jute	–.38	–.22	–.02	–.54	–0.56							
Sisal	.15	–.44	–.22	.82	–.13	–0.41						
Rubber	.09	.39	.82	–.28	.45	–.10	–0.02					
Copper	0	0	–.44	–.25	–.28	.47	–.21	–0.41				
Tin	.06	–.39	–.55	0	–.27	.23	–.12	–.47	0.50			
Wheat	.41	–.32	–.39	.62	.32	–.39	.79	–.07	.08	0.13		
Rice	.54	–.39	–.52	.41	.08	–.18	.47	–.29	.32	.38	0.82	
Wool	.06	.19	.16	.15	.58	0	.13	.37	–.16	–.34	.53	0.20

Sources: International Bank for Reconstruction and Development, *Commodity Trade and Price Trends* (1975); United Nations, Food and Agriculture Organization, *Trade Yearbook* (1974); United Nations, *Monthly Bulletin of Statistics*, March, 1976. The price series used and the deflator were those identified in table 2-3.

Table 3-3
UNCTAD Secretariat Estimates of Handling and Storage Costs for Ten Commodities

Commodity	*Handling Costs (Dollars per ton)*[a]	*Storage Cost (Dollars per Ton-Year)*[b]	*Costs of Storing the Maximum Stock for One Year, Plus Handling Costs ($ millions)*[c]
Coffee	14.33	32.82	28.2
Cocoa	3.76	24.27	21.6
Tea	6.61	32.18	5.0
Sugar	11.35	24.80	224.9
Cotton	7.16	17.67	15.8
Jute	7.05	12.12	11.0
Sisal	5.04	11.11	3.2
Rubber	5.51	27.78	29.2
Copper	3.48	7.08	12.0
Tin	4.85	7.27	0.6

Source: United Nations Conference on Trade and Development, "Common Fund: Financial Requirements," note by the UNCTAD Secretariat, TD/B/IPC/CF/L.2, December 29, 1976, table A.4, p. 9. The original figures were stated in terms of metric tons.

[a]Handling costs per ton for movements into or out of warehouses.

[b]Cost of deadweight storage plus costs of rotation.

[c]Storage costs plus twice handling costs times the stock requirement from table 3-1.

there for one year, and then moving it out again. The total of these values for the ten commodities is $351.5 million (64 percent of which is accounted for by sugar), or 4.8 percent of estimated capital requirements without pooling ($7.3 billion). These figures provide only a very rough notion of handling and storage costs because a buffer stock would not hold the maximum quantity at all times but material acquired would sometimes be held for more than one year.

A buffer stock would be required to buy at a floor price and sell at a higher ceiling price, which opens up the possibility of a trading profit (an excess of revenues from sales over expenditures for purchases). A trading profit in even this limited sense is not guaranteed. In particular, if the floor price is set above the long-run competitive equilibrium price, it is unlikely that significant sales at the ceiling price would be made. Furthermore, a stock acquired early in a recession might have to be held for two or three years before it could be sold at the ceiling price, and loan financing might be very difficult to arrange in such circumstances. However, there is a presumption that a skillfully and prudently managed buffer stock would make a trading profit.

The UNCTAD Secretariat study provides estimates of the trading profits less operating costs (but not capital costs) for buffer stocks in the ten core commodities. This study used the costs of handling and storage given in table

3-3. Administrative costs were assumed to be 0.5 percent of capital invested during the year, and costs of insurance, pilferage, deterioration of the stock, and so forth were assumed to be 1.0 percent of invested capital. Finally, the present value of gains and losses in the value of the stock plus cash were considered. For the 1979-1983 period, the estimated rates of return ranged from a low of 3.8 percent for sugar to a high of 8.6 percent for tin. The weighted average rate of return for the ten commodities was 6.8 percent before capital costs.[7]

The U.S. Treasury study of buffer stocks for copper and tin provides a less optimistic view of trading profits. Storage costs were assumed to be 0.25 percent of the value of the stock held during the year; transaction costs were assumed to be 1 percent of the value of purchases; and a discount rate of 2 percent was assumed. Net trading profit was defined in the same way as it was in the UNCTAD study but stated in terms of present value rather than a rate of return. Given these assumptions, it was estimated that a copper buffer stock designed to maintain price with ±10 percent of a five-year moving average of past prices would have had annual average losses of $13 million, or about 0.2 percent of capital requirements. Under the same trading rule, it was estimated that a tin buffer stock would have had a small trading profit over the nineteen-year period.[8] These estimates are not unfavorable to buffer stocks, however. Although the available evidence is too thin to support firm conclusions, it seems that the trading profit of a well-managed buffer stock would, on average, be about equal to administrative, storage, and handling costs.

Direct Benefits of Buffer Stocks

The principal economic benefits claimed for buffer stocks are improved growth prospects for the LDCs resulting from reduced fluctuations in their export earnings, a lower rate of inflation in the DCs, lower costs of production for commodities and hence lower average prices, and increased profits to suppliers and/or buyers because of reduced fluctuations in prices. Only the last of these will be examined here. This choice reflects two conclusions reached in chapter 2. First, the magnitude of the direct benefits to reducing price fluctuations is a significant consideration in the choice between compensatory financing and buffer stocks. Second, it seems unlikely that buffer stocks would have a marked effect on inflation in the DCs or on the costs of producing commodities.

Figure 3-3 will be used to identify the direct gains and losses to price stabilization.[9] Short-run supply is assumed to be S_1 in good crop years and S_2 in bad crop years. Unlike figure 2-1, short-run supply is not assumed to be completely inelastic and long-run supply is not shown. It is understood that a buffer stock would buy to maintain price $\overline{P}$ in good crop years and sell to maintain $\overline{P}$ in bad crop years.

The upper panel of figure 3-3 shows the effect of the buffer stock's

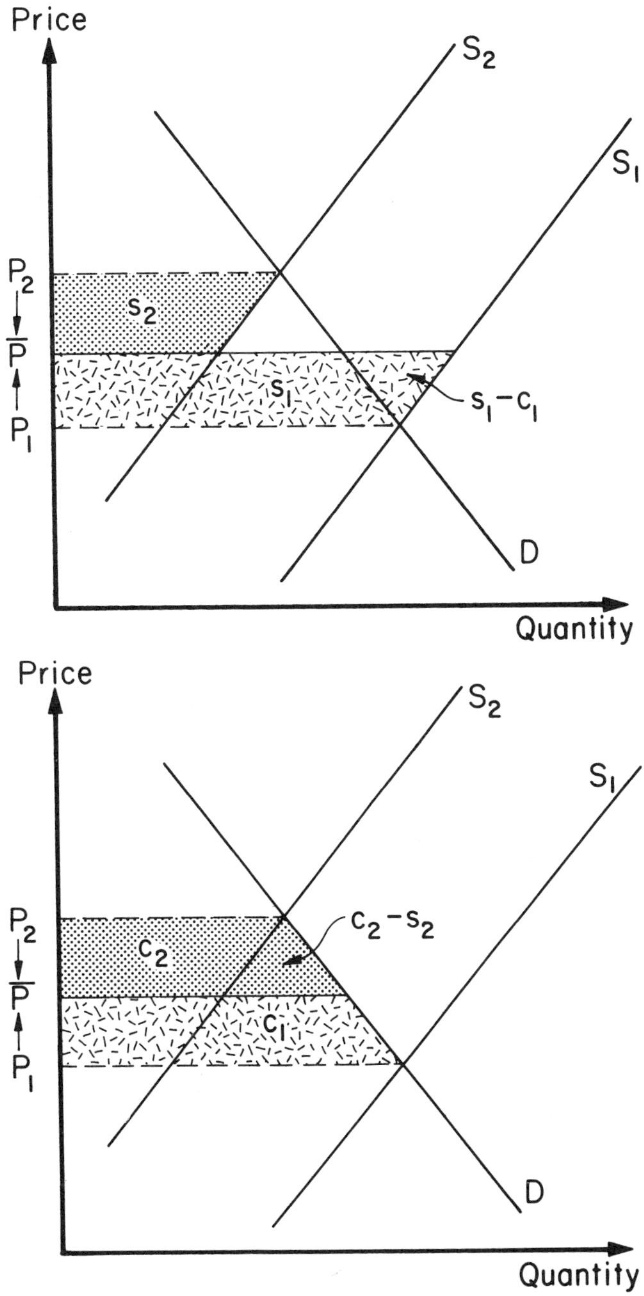

Figure 3-3. Gains to Suppliers and Buyers from Price Stabilization When Only Supply Varies

activities on suppliers. Suppliers' revenue is price times quantity, and the total cost of producing any output q is equal to the area under the supply curve to q. It can be seen, then, that because of the buffer stock sales, suppliers lose profits equal in magnitude to the area s_2. In good crop years, the buffer stock would buy to support price $\overline{P}$, which would increase suppliers' profit by an amount equal to the area s_1. The total gain to suppliers from price stabilization is $G_s = s_1 - s_2$, and it is clear that s_1 is larger than s_2, so suppliers gain by price stabilization when demand is stable and supply varies. The lower panel of figure 3-3 presents a similar analysis for buyers. If buyers are interpreted as final consumers, the appropriate measure of gains and losses is consumers' surplus, which is measured here by the area under the demand curve less expenditure.[10] Increasing price to $\overline{P}$ reduces consumers' surplus by an amount equal to the area labeled c_1, and when the buffer stock acts to hold price down to $\overline{P}$, consumers gain an amount equal to the area c_2. The net gain to consumers is $G_c = c_2 - c_1$, and it is clear from the figure that c_1 exceeds c_2, so consumers are net losers from price stabilization if supply varies while demand is constant.

The total gain to consumers and producers as a group is

$$G_T = (c_2 - c_1) + (s_1 - s_2). \tag{3.3}$$

Rearranging terms:

$$G_T = (c_2 - s_2) + (s_1 - c_1). \tag{3.4}$$

The first term in this expression is the net gain to consumers and producers as a group when the buffer stock sells to reduce price from P_1 to $\overline{P}$. Looking back at figure 3-3 it is clear that c_2 is greater than s_2 (consumers gain more by the price reduction than suppliers lose). The second term in figure 3-3 is the net gain when price is supported, and, again it is clear that suppliers gain more than consumers lose when the buffer stock acts to support price at $\overline{P}$. Since both terms are positive, there are net gains from price stabilization to buyers and sellers as a group.

A second relevant case is shown in figure 3-4, where it is assumed that supply is stable but demand varies. The buffer stock again is assumed trade so as to stabilize price at its average value $\overline{P}$. For this case, arguments that parallel those used above lead to these conclusions:

1. Consumers are net gainers and suppliers are net losers from price stabilization.
2. Consumers gain more than suppliers lose when price is held down, and suppliers gain more than consumers lose when price is supported.
3. There are net gains to buyers and sellers as a group from price stabilization.

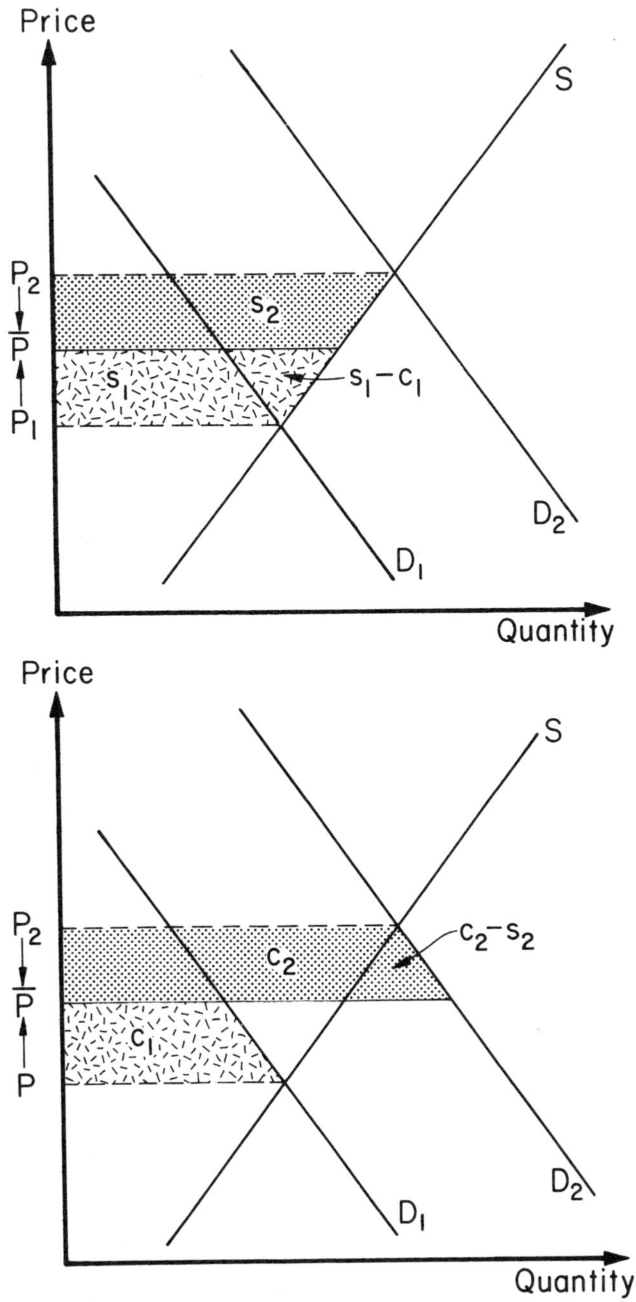

Figure 3-4. Gains to Suppliers and Buyers from Price Stabilization When Only Demand Varies

In the general case where both supply and demand vary, both buyers and sellers may be net gainers. However, suppliers may be net gainers while consumers are net losers, or consumers may gain while suppliers lose. The nature of the outcome, in this case, depends on the elasticities of supply and demand, the magnitude of variation in supply and demand, and the correlation between shifts in supply and demand. The only general statement that can be made is that there are net gains from price stabilization to buyers and sellers as a group.[11]

It is necessary at this point to ask why, if there are net gains from reducing price fluctuations, private buffer stocks do not exist. Suppose, for the sake of the argument, that a privately held buffer stock for some commodity is in existence and that its activities in reducing price fluctuations provide direct benefits to suppliers and/or buyers. Since price fluctuations could not be reduced for only some traders, all buyers and sellers would receive the benefits of the buffer stock whether or not they contributed to its costs. They would, accordingly, have no incentive to contribute to the costs of the buffer stock and presumably would not do so. This argument, which is an example of what is called a free rider problem, explains why buffer stocks might not exist even though their direct benefits to buyers and sellers exceed their costs.[12]

Table 3-4 presents illustrative values of the expected (or average) annual gains to price stabilization for each of the three cases identified. (The assumptions used in making these computations are stated in appendix A.) Briefly, the computations rest on values for the elasticities of supply and demand, actual price and quantity for 1971, and hypothetical variations in supply and demand. It was assumed that variations in each of supply and demand alone are sufficient to cause a ±10 percent variation in sales from the base level.

The first ten commodities listed in table 3-4 are those of the core group in the UNCTAD Integrated Programme. For the case in which both supply and demand vary, annual average gains for these commodities to suppliers and buyers are \$277.4 million and \$386.0 million, respectively, and total gains for the ten commodities are \$663.4 million. These figures are not impressively large, particularly since sugar accounts for nearly 50 percent of each of the totals. It may also be relevant to note that the costs of even very modest increases in the average level of commodity prices would exceed the estimated value to buyers of reducing price fluctuations (compare with table 4-2).

Comparison of Benefits and Costs

The benefit figures that appear in table 3-4 assume that prices are maintained at exactly the long-run competitive equilibrium and are, for that reason, not comparable to the cost estimates discussed earlier. It is possible, however, to use essentially the model used for table 3-4 to estimate maximum capital requirements and thereby produce a rudimentary cost benefit analysis of buffer stocks.

Table 3-4
Expected Annual Gains from Price Stabilization
(Millions of Dollars)

	Supply Varies			Demand Varies			Both Vary		
Commodity	*Producers*	*Consumers*	*Total*	*Producers*	*Consumers*	*Total*	*Producers*	*Consumers*	*Total*
Cocoa	21.4	−7.0	14.5	−7.5	21.9	14.5	14.0	14.9	28.9
Coffee	28.6	−8.9	19.7	−10.8	30.6	19.7	17.7	21.7	39.4
Tea	8.2	−2.1	6.1	−4.0	10.1	6.1	4.1	8.0	12.2
Cotton	25.8	−5.6	20.3	−14.7	34.9	20.3	11.2	29.4	40.5
Sugar	226.0	−67.0	159.0	−92.1	251.1	159.0	133.9	184.2	318.1
Jute	1.6	−0.6	1.0	−0.4	1.4	1.0	1.2	0.7	2.0
Sisal	2.2	−0.9	1.3	−0.4	1.8	1.3	1.8	0.9	2.7
Rubber	15.2	−6.4	8.8	−2.4	11.2	8.8	12.8	4.8	17.6
Copper	114.0	−31.9	82.1	−50.2	132.3	82.1	63.9	100.4	164.2
Tin	27.3	−8.4	18.9	−10.5	29.4	18.9	16.8	21.0	37.8
Wool	153.0	−50.3	102.7	−52.4	155.1	102.7	100.6	104.8	205.4
Wheat	105.1	−18.9	86.2	−67.2	153.4	86.2	37.9	134.5	172.3
Rice	324.2	−60.8	263.4	−202.7	466.1	263.4	121.6	405.3	526.9

Source: See appendix A to this book.

The results obtained appear in the first column of table 3-5. It was assumed that both supply and demand vary and that variations in supply or demand alone are sufficient to produce ±10 percent fluctuations in output from the base level and that the buffer stock trades so as to maintain exactly the target price. For comparison, estimated capital requirements are also shown on the assumption that the buffer stock trades so as to keep price within ±10 percent of the target. Appendix A presents the other assumptions used and explains the computations in detail.

Moving from capital requirements to capital costs requires some information about the appropriate discount rate, which depends on the opportunity cost of funds to the buffer stock, the rate at which the buffer stock can lend, and the average amount of funds committed to stocks. If the opportunity cost of capital were 15 percent and the buffer stock could lend at 6 percent and its funds were committed two-thirds of the time, the appropriate discount rate would be 8 percent. Adding 2 percent for administrative costs, storage, and so forth, average

Table 3-5
Direct Benefits to Reducing Price Fluctuations and 5 Percent and 10 Percent of Capital Requirements for a Simple Model in Which Supply and Demand Vary
(Millions of Dollars)

Commodity	*Estimated Capital Requirements*		*Fraction of Capital Requirements for f = 0*		*Direct Benefits to Suppliers and Buyers*	*Direct Benefits Minus 5 Percent of Capital Requirement for f = 0*[b]
	f = 0[a]	*f = 0.1*	*0.05*	*0.10*		
Cocoa	1,077	894	53.6	107.7	28.9	–24.7
Coffee	1,433	1,221	71.7	143.3	39.4	–32.3
Tea	377	337	18.9	37.7	12.2	–6.7
Sugar	7,271	6,582	363.6	727.1	318.1	–45.5
Cotton	3,009	2,425	150.5	300.9	40.5	–110.0
Jute	101	82	5.1	10.1	2.0	–3.1
Sisal	81	72	4.1	8.1	2.7	–1.4
Rubber	1,019	940	51.0	101.9	17.6	–33.4
Copper	3,732	3,413	170.7	341.3	164.2	–6.5
Tin	414	395	19.3	39.5	37.8	18.5
Wool	6,040	4,666	233.3	466.6	205.4	–27.9
Wheat	13,714	13,102	655.1	1310.2	172.3	–428.8
Rice	11,569	10,562	528.1	1056.2	526.9	–1.2

Source: Appendix A to this book.
[a]*f*: permitted variation in price from target
[b]From table 3-4; benefits to buyers and sellers when both supply and demand vary.

annual costs would be 10 percent of capital requirements. If the opportunity cost were 9 percent and the other costs remain unchanged, costs would be 6 percent of capital requirements per year. The values shown in table 3-5 then span the range of likely capital costs.

Estimated direct benefits exceed 5 percent of capital requirements for tin. In all other cases, estimated direct benefits are less than 5 percent of capital requirements, although only very slightly less for rice.

Pooling puts buffer stocks in a more favorable light. For the first ten commodities listed in table 3-5, benefits are $245 million (or 27 percent), less than 5 percent of capital costs, and if cotton is excluded, these figures become $135 million and 18 percent. The information presented earlier suggests that pooling could well reduce capital requirements by enough to make buffer stocks marginally profitable if net capital changes are 5 percent. This figure, however, is somewhat optimistic, and direct benefits (excluding cotton) are only 41 percent of estimated costs at 10 percent. In this case, even if pooling reduced capital requirements by 25 percent, estimated annual benefits for the ten commodities would be about $514 million less than costs.

This analysis rests on assumptions that are reasonable but not beyond question, and it is possible that more detailed studies would produce different results. But to the extent that the evidence of this example is accepted, it seems that with few exceptions, buffer stocks' direct benefits are insufficient to justify their costs. With this, the discussion comes back to the conclusions of the preceding chapter.

Chapter 2 provided two tests of whether buffer stocks would be less expensive than compensatory financing as a way of limiting declines in the LDCs' export earnings: the fraction of the commodity exported by the LDCs and the magnitude of direct benefits to reducing price fluctuations. For all but three of the core commodities, the LDCs' share of the world market exceeds 80 percent (see table 4-2). The exceptions are cotton, copper, and sugar, and for the latter two the comparison between direct benefits and costs is relatively favorable. It seems, then, that each of the core commodities, except perhaps cotton, would pass the tests stated in chapter 2. This is a very limited conclusion, however. The issue is whether the indirect effects of buffer stocks, and especially the benefits of limiting sharp declines in the LDCs' export earnings, are, together with direct benefits, sufficient to justify the costs of buffer stocks.

The figures in table 3-5 provide some help in forming this problem. The difference between direct benefits and capital costs can be regarded as an annual average premium on (partial) insurance against declines in the LDCs' export earnings. Under the most favorable assumptions, the premium might be a small positive return; under the least favorable assumptions, the premium could run up to $500 million.

This way of formulating the problem leads to the question of how much insurance buffer stocks in the ten core commodities would provide. It would be ideal to have estimates of the effects of buffer stocks in the ten core commodities on the degree of instability in the export earnings of each of the LDCs, but such estimates are not available and could be constructed only with great difficulty. As a substitute, table 3-6 provides information on the fraction of LDCs' export earnings accounted for by the ten core commodities. These figures give a crude indication of the extent to which reducing fluctuations in earnings from the ten core commodities would reduce fluctuations in each country's total export earnings. However, they cannot be translated into even an overall qualitative assessment of the amount of insurance that buffer stocks in the ten core commodities would provide. All that can be said is that the insurance would range from nearly complete coverage for a few LDCs to virtually none at all for nearly half of the LDCs.

It is not obvious that, given their capital costs, buffer stocks in the ten core commodities provide the greatest possible insurance against declines in the LDCs' export earnings. There might be some other set of commodities that from the point of view of stabilizing the LDCs' export earnings would be better. The pooling argument introduces a related complication. Some commodity might have an unfavorable cost/benefit ratio when considered in isolation but look much better as part of a set of related buffer stocks. Unfortunately, the problem of selecting an optimal set of commodities for buffer stocks goes far beyond what can be considered here.

Taking the ten core commodities as given, there is still a question of whether the value of the insurance that they provide is, along with the magnitude of direct benefits, sufficient to warrant creation of buffer stocks in them. Although, given the state of empirical research on the effects of instability in export earnings, this is largely a matter of judgment, the figures in table 3-5 make it easy to believe that buffer stocks for several of the core commodities could be economically justified. This does not imply, however, that buffer stocks in the ten core commodities, instead of other commodities, would provide the best insurance against declines in the LDCs' export earnings or that the funds required to create buffer stocks could not be better spent in some other way.

Taken as a whole, this discussion warrants three conclusions. First, there is no general case for buffer stocks. Buffer stocks in the ten core commodities would not stabilize the LDCs' export earnings but would provide varying degrees of protection against declines in export earnings to about half of the LDCs. Second, buffer stocks for several of the core commodities probably could be economically justified. The third conclusion, which is really a qualification on the second, is that a solid economic case for buffer stocks in the ten core commodities has not been made.

Table 3-6
Percent of Total Export Earnings Obtained by LDCs from Exports of the Ten Core Commodities in the Integrated Programme for Commodities, Average, 1970-1972

Country	*Earnings from Core Commodities*	*Country*	*Earnings from Core Commodities*
Zambia	94.1%	Dahomey	44.7%
Uganda	92.6	Brazil	43.1
Mauritius	88.7	Nicaragua	42.3
Rivanda	80.7	Tanzania	40.8
Equatorial Guinea	78.1	Syrian Arab Republic	39.3
Zäire	76.6	Peru	38.9
Sri Lanka	75.4	Angola	36.9
Chile	72.0	Yemen Arab Republic	36.0
Cuba	72.0	Barbados	35.6
Columbia	66.7	Philippines	34.4
Dominican Republic	65.0	Mali	33.9
Chad	62.5	Malagasy Republic	32.9
Ghana	61.4	Ecuador	31.4
Sudan	60.6	Guyana	31.1
Bangladesh	59.8	Indonesia	30.0
Togo	57.2	Belize	29.9
Cameroon	57.0	Thailand	28.3
Bolivia	56.8	Mozambique	28.2
Ethiopia	55.5	British West Indies	28.1
Fiji	55.5	Mexico	22.3
Papua New Guinea	55.5	Upper Volta	21.7
Haiti	54.8	Liberia	18.2
Guadalupe	52.7	El Salvadore	16.7
Ivory Coast	52.2	Pakistan	16.2
Central Africa Republic	52.1	Honduras	16.0
Republic of Vietnam	52.1	Nigeria	14.3
Kenya	48.1	India	14.2
Egypt	48.0	Afghanistan	13.9
Guatemala	46.8	Khmer Republic	12.9
Malaysia	46.5	Jamaica	11.0
		Burma	6.3

Source: Compiled from data in International Bank for Reconstruction and Development, *Commodity Trade and Price Trends* (1975).

Note: A number of countries not shown obtain small fractions of their export earnings from one or more of the ten core commodities.

Aspects of Buffer Stock Management

Even if a case for buffer stocks is made on the basis of a cost/benefit analysis, there would be questions about whether a buffer stock would behave as it is intended to and would avoid disastrous mistakes. There is, however, virtually no historical experience against which this assumption can be tested, and the operation of a buffer stock clearly involves some problems.[13]

The trading rules of a buffer stock would be essentially as follows:

1. When market price falls below the floor price, buy to support the floor price, committing all available funds if necessary.
2. When market price rises above the ceiling price, sell as required to maintain the ceiling price, exhausting the entire stock held if necessary.

The floor and ceiling prices would be tied to a target price, and purchases and sales would balance over the course of a few years if the target price is correctly chosen. If, however, the target price is set too high, the buffer stock becomes an attempt at a price support program.

The consequences of attempting to maintain too high a target price and bad luck are illustrated by the fate of a valorization scheme undertaken by Brazil. In 1923, Brazil established the Coffee Defense Institute. The institute advanced payment to the producers, based on a preestablished price, when their crops were delivered to government warehouses. The base price should have been set at the average level of price over good and bad years. Instead, it was maintained above this level, especially after 1926, so the valorization scheme became a price support program. The Coffee Defense Institute was able to handle the bumper harvest of 1927-1928, but when another large crop followed in 1929, contrary to the usual cycle, the institute was unable to obtain sufficient financing and was forced to stop buying. Coffee prices then declined by approximately 50 percent.[14] In this case, the target price was maintained at what proved to be too high a level. The same mistake could be made in the operation of a buffer stock, and a buffer stock might also be led into an attempt at price support by a failure to adjust the target price appropriately.

It is easy to identify situations in which this would tend to occur. Suppose, for example, that a technological improvement of a substitute product results in a large decrease in demand. The market adjustments that would occur in this situation are as follows:

1. Price would initially fall below long-run average cost.
2. All suppliers would incur losses on a long-term basis; marginal suppliers might be forced out immediately; there would be no new entry; and existing capacity would not be replaced as it wore out.
3. As supply fell, price would rise toward long-run average cost.

4. A new equilibrium would eventually be established with price equal to long-run average cost but with consumption and supply reduced in accord with the lower level of demand.

If the decline in demand were temporary, the buffer stock should purchase so as to support price at the preset lower bound. However, given that the demand is permanent, an attempt to support the price would slow down the adjustment process and lead to an ever-increasing stock.

Technological change that reduces cost presents a similar problem. Once the new technology was introduced on a significant scale, price would tend to fall toward the average cost with the new technology, which is, by hypothesis, less than the average cost with the old. Suppliers using the old technology would lose money and would continue to do so until they left the market or adopted the new technology. The buffer stock should not attempt to support the price.

A large increase in operating cost while demand remains constant provides a third and probably more commonly encountered problem. In this case, price would initially rise, but by less than the amount of the increase in average cost, so all firms would experience losses. The adjustment to long-run equilibrium then proceeds as in the first example. In this situation, it would clearly be wrong to attempt to hold price down, and it is more likely that managers of a buffer stock would be under pressure to recognize the full impact of the cost increase in the target price, which would eliminate the incentive to reduce capacity. The correct response for the buffer stock is to do nothing and let price rise.

The common element of these three examples is the need for a reduction in capacity. If the ICO blindly defended price bounds, it would thwart the required changes and, as a result, accumulate a large stock. It is assumed here that the buffer stock would have a fixed budget and would have no power to restrict supply. Given these limitations, the buffer stock would not permanently maintain price above the competitive equilibrium. The dangers are that the buffer stock would collapse financially or would become fully committed and hence unable to trade so as to reduce price fluctuations.

These dangers arise because the long-run competitive equilibrium price cannot be easily observed. The prices established day by day and the trend in prices over a period of months or years give an indication of the long-run equilibrium price, but there is no simple formula that measures the long-run equilibrium price. The long-run equilibrium price equals the long-run average cost of efficient operations, and in simple situations it may be possible to measure the relevant costs, but this is not usually a practical possibility.

The problem of setting the target price is not, however, quite so intractable as these comments suggest, since the market would provide evidence of mistakes. If the target price were set below long-run average cost, production would decline and the price could not be held once the stock was exhuasted. If price were set above long-run average cost, supply would exceed demand. When the buffer stock reached the limit of its ability to purchase excess supply, price would fall. If these signals are correctly perceived and acted upon, small errors in setting the target price are tolerable.

An obvious way to exploit these facts is to set the target price as a moving average of past market prices.[15] Use of a moving average of past market prices might be justified on the grounds that it measures the long-run equilibrium price. This justification, however, is weak, since long-run adjustments typically require several years to complete. The principal reason for using a moving average of past market prices is simply that doing so guarantees that the buffer stock would accommodate itself to long-run shifts in the market rather than attempt to override them.

The use of a moving average rule only partially solves the problems created by permanent shifts in the market. In the face of a large decrease in the level of demand or a large increase in supply, the rules of the buffer stock would more or less automatically trigger purchases, and the buffer stock could well become fully committed. If the changes are transitory, this is appropriate. But if the changes are permanent, the buffer stock would be unable to sell for several years and, during this period, would be out of the business of trading to reduce price fluctuations. The use of a moving average rule would prevent a situation such as this from persisting, but it would not prevent its occurrence. To avoid the situation, the buffer stock would have to possess the analytical capability to diagnose permanent shifts in the market and the right to reduce the target price immediately in the appropriate circumstances.

To summarize, four safeguards should be built into a buffer stock. First, the buffer stock should have a fixed budget. Second, the target price should be set as a moving average of past market prices. Third, which is a matter of definition, a pure buffer stock involves no restrictions on supply. Fourth, the buffer stock should have the ability to recognize and the power to stand aside from permanent shifts in the market. If these rules are observed, a buffer stock could not maintain price above the competitive equilibrium level and would have a reasonable chance of maintaining the ability to trade so as to reduce fluctuations in price.

These comments have been directed to the operating rules and problems of a pure buffer stock. The difficulties that arise at that level seem to be capable of solution. Whether the members of an ICO would be willing to leave a buffer stock on autopilot is a question of a different sort and one that cannot be answered conclusively. But if a buffer stock is to be limited to the task of reducing price fluctuations, its rules must be appropriately structured and the limited character of a buffer stock be understood and accepted.

Concluding Comments

Although the computations presented here are too crude to support definite conclusions, it seems likely that buffer stocks would be economical propositions for several commodities. However, their potential importance is limited by their nature. A pure buffer stock would serve only to reduce period-to-period fluctuations in price, suppliers' incomes, and buyers' expenditures. Although this effect may be useful, the results would not be large. It seems to be unlikely that a system of pure buffer stocks would have profound effects on the LDCs or would work sweeping changes in world commodity trade.

Notes

1. U.S., Treasury, *U.S. Commodity Policy* (Washington, D.C.: Office of Raw Materials and Oceans Policy, Treasury Department, February 1976), p. 61.
2. Ibid., pp. 74-75.
3. Ibid., pp. 65-66.
4. I am indebted to Bruce Benton for pointing this out to me.
5. A correlation coefficient must be in the interval of −1 to +1 inclusive. A value of +1 indicates perfect positive correlation, and a value of −1 perfect negative correlation.
6. UNCTAD, "Common Fund: Financial Requirements," note by the UNCTAD Secretariat, TD/B/IPC/CF/L.2, December 29, 1976, table 3, pp. 13-14.
7. Ibid., table 4, p. 19.
8. U.S. Treasury, *U.S. Commodity Policy*, pp. 65-67, 74-76.
9. The argument presented here follows B.F. Massell, "Price Stabilization and Welfare," *Quarterly Journal of Economics* 83 (1969):285-298.
10. The rationale of this definition is basically as follows. Suppose that purchases are made on a monthly basis and that demand remains stable over several months. Assume that price is 100 in month 1 and 90 in month 2 and that the quantity demanded is 1 unit in month 1 and 2 units in month 2. Expenditure is then 100 in month 1 and 180 in month 2. In month 2, the first unit is purchased for 90; but from the results of month 1, it is clear that the consumer places a value of at least 100 on the first unit bought. Hence, the total value placed on the 2 units must be at least 180 + 10 = 190, so consumers' surplus is at least 10. If price were reduced in smaller increments, it would become clear that the change in consumers' surplus is an area such as c_2 in figure 3-3.
11. See Stephen J. Turnovsky, "The Distribution of the Welfare Gains from Price Stabilization: The Case of Multiplicative Disturbances," *International Economic Review* 17 (1976):133-148.
12. The market cannot be entirely ignored, however. Under some conditions, which are difficult to interpret, the futures market or private savings may provide insurance that is superior to that of a buffer stock. On this question, see R. McKinnon, "Futures Markets, Buffer Stocks, and Income Stability for Primary Producers," *Journal of Political Economy* 65 (1967):844-861, and B.F. Massell, "Some Welfare Implications of International Price Stabilization," *Journal of Political Economy* 68 (1970):404-417. On the related question of

whether speculation is stabilizing, see Milton Friedman, *Essays in Positive Economies* (Chicago: University of Chicago Press, 1953), William Baumol, "Speculation, Profitability and Stability," *Review of Economics and Statistics* 39 (1957):263-271, and Harry G. Johnson, "Destabilizing Speculation: A General Equilibrium Approach," *Journal of Political Economy* 84 (1976):109-122.

13. The experience of the International Tin Council is of limited relevance since its buffer stock is small and the tin agreement has relied primarily on export controls.

14. J.W.F. Rowe, *Primary Commodities in International Trade* (Cambridge: Cambridge University Press, 1965), pp. 133-136, argues that the valorization program was brought down in 1929 because of the bad luck of two good harvests in succession and that the scheme would have failed within a few years in any event because too high a price was maintained.

15. J.M. Keynes, "The International Control of Raw Materials," *Journal of International Economics* 4 (1974):303, suggested that revisions of the target price be governed by rules relating the level (or rate of change) of the stock to desired levels or rates of change.

4 Restrictive Commodity Arrangements

Buffer stocks are not an established feature of international commodity agreements. In fact, of the eighteen major agreements made during the past half-century, only the prewar and postwar tin agreements operated a buffer stock, and neither of these was a pure buffer stock.[1] The principal mechanism of commodity agreements has been, and continues to be, restriction on supply.

Export quotas and production controls have a somewhat murky status in discussions of price stabilization. On the one hand, a restriction of supply is often classified, with some historical justification, as a stabilization measure. But a restriction is also a monopolistic device, and its use need not be limited to the modest objective of avoiding episodes of very low prices.

The United States has consistently opposed the use of commodity agreements as a means of transferring income to the LDCs. Some would argue that the Integrated Programme on Commodities (IPC) is not designed to increase commodity prices. This raises the question, Why discuss restrictive agreements? There are two answers. First, the LDCs as a bloc and some of the DCs are in favor of using commodity agreements as a means of transferring income to the LDCs. Second, whatever is said about these objectives, commodity agreements typically contain mechanisms capable of increasing commodity prices at least for a time, and so a study of restrictive measures provides a useful perspective on some of the ambiguities of the IPC.

Mechanisms of Restrictive Commodity Agreements

There is nothing distinctive about the legal form of a restrictive commodity agreement. It is a treaty among importing and exporting nations, which would create an international commodity organization (ICO) and grant it specified powers for a fixed period. The ICO would have a professional staff and a governing board made up of representatives of member nations responsible for making policy decisions. All of these would also be said of a pure buffer stock arrangement. The defining features of restrictive arrangements lie in the powers granted to the ICO and the way in which it uses those powers.

Attention is often focused directly on price, which is inappropriate because the prices of most commodities are determined on open markets. In these cases, an agreement on price is literally meaningless, since the market price adjusts to equate the quantities demanded and supplied. The key element of a restrictive arrangement is a means for controlling supply.

Export quotas are the most common (but not the only) form of supply restriction. Some agreements have coupled export quotas with controls on inventories, and a few have attempted to regulate production in addition to or in place of limitations on exports. These distinctions, however, are not crucial to the discussion that follows.

The process of restricting supply revolves around a specification of each supplier's base or standard exports, which is usually written into the agreement and holds for its life. When total exports are cut back, each supplier's exports are cut back proportionally. In effect, market shares are established, and then total exports are adjusted as is deemed appropriate.

The administration of a system of export quotas requires decisions on when to impose quotas, the duration of quotas, and the stringency of the quotas. Some aspects of these decisions are usually specified by the agreement, but a measure of the responsibility would be retained by the ICO's governing body. Decisions at this level are usually established by a complex voting procedure, which requires a majority of both exporters and importers, considered as separate groups, for positive action. Although deadlocks are clearly a possibility, too much weight should not be placed on voting procedures. Decisions on export quotas are basically a matter for negotiation among the member nations within a preestablished framework.

The member nations of a restrictive arrangement would bind themselves to observe export quotas, but it would be naive to assume that a system of export quotas is self-policing. In fact, overshipping is common and, accordingly, a policing mechanism will usually be required if the system is to be successful. Past commodity agreements, when they have attempted to enforce quotas, have used one of two mechanisms. The first of these is a "free zone" (an area in which members and nonmembers alike may sell as much of the commodity as they choose). The second mechanism is a certificate system, which relies on the customs services of importing nations to enforce export quotas.

No mention has so far been made of a buffer stock. A buffer stock might be convenient for various reasons and might provide benefits to buyers, which could be important politically, but a buffer stock is not a necessary ingredient of a restrictive commodity agreement. The crucial mechanisms of a restrictive arrangement are a means for establishing restrictions on supply and a mechanism for enforcing the restrictions on supply. These powers would permit an ICO to increase price above the competitive level, at least temporarily.

Potential Effects of Restrictive Agreements

The success of restrictive commodity agreements is not assured. The organization could collapse or be reduced to impotence by internal conflicts, for example. Even if these problems are laid aside, the increase in earnings that a restrictive commodity agreement could generate is limited by the size of the markets and the characteristics of demand and production costs.

Table 4-1 presents very rough estimates of the effects of price increases for sixteen commodities. The values shown assume that the demand for each of the commodities was at its 1971 level. The estimates take account of the fact that price increases reduce consumption and incorporate a crude attempt to take account of the effect of reductions in the quantity produced on the costs of production. However, it must be stressed that these figures have no more than indicative significance.

The demand elasticities used in the computation were constant and less than 1 in absolute value, which, if true for the entire range, would imply that revenue and profit are maximized by indefinitely large prices. Rather than attempt to adjust the elasticities for changes in price, price increases of +20 percent and +100 percent were assumed. A doubling of prices may seem modest in the light of OPEC's achievements, but the historical record indicates that it would be a monumental success. Furthermore, since short-run elasticities were used, only substitution that occurs within one year is considered, and, for some commodities, substitution required several years to accomplish.[2] For this reason, the estimates in table 4-1 should be regarded as maximal.

Table 4-1
Estimated Effects of Price Increases on Revenue and Profit
(Millions of Dollars)

	20 Percent Increase in Price		*100 Percent Increase in Price*	
Commodity	*Increase in Revenue*	*Increase in Profit*	*Increase in Revenue*	*Increase in Profit*
Cocoa	390	570	1,950	2,870
Coffee	520	710	2,590	3,550
Tea	140	170	720	860
Sugar	3,050	3,630	15,230	18,100
Cotton	870	1,190	4,350	5,960
Jute	24	47	118	236
Sisal	25	36	126	180
Rubber	174	290	869	1,448
Copper	1,525	1,774	7,627	8,868
Tin	188	204	904	1,022
Bananas	33	132	165	660
Bauxite	187	191	936	956
Iron ore	556	618	2,782	3,091

Source: Appendix A to this book.

Given the 1971 level of demand and the other assumptions made, a 20 percent increase in the price of each of the ten core commodities would generate an additional revenue of $6.9 billion, and a 100 percent price increase would increase revenues by approximately $34.5 billion. It is worth adding that copper and sugar account for about two-thirds of each of these values.

The LDCs would not obtain all of any increase in revenue and would pay part of the increased prices. These two effects are described by the estimates presented in table 4-2. The first column of this table shows the fraction of the commodity exported by the LDCs. It is reasonable to assume that if the LDCs export, say, 90 percent of a commodity, they would obtain 90 percent of any increase in revenue due to higher prices. The figures in columns 2 and 3 use this assumption and the estimates given in table 4-1 to compute the revenue flows to the LDCs from higher prices for the thirteen commodities. Columns 4-6 present estimates of the increased costs to the LDCs of higher commodity prices, and the final column shows the net revenue flows to the LDCs. The net increase in revenue to the LDCs for 20 percent and 100 percent increases in the prices of the ten core commodities would be $3.8 billion and $18.9 billion, respectively.

These overall figures mask the fact that some of the LDCs would be net losers if commodity prices were increased. The principal gainers would be the major producers of cocoa, coffee, cotton, copper, and sugar. Approximately thirty of the LDCs would be in this group. The losers would be nations that export relatively low value commodities and that import substantial quantities of other commodities, especially cotton, copper, and sugar. The data on commodity imports required to identify these nations are not available, but quantitative information provides some help. India, Bangladesh, the nations just below the Sahara, and many of the nations in northern Africa and Southeast Asia export relatively low value crops, and there is some indication that they tend to be importers of agricultural products. These nations, which are the majority of the poorest of the LDCs, would probably be net losers under a system of restrictive commodity agreements.

The information in table 4-3 provides a way of putting the estimates of table 4-2 in perspective. In 1972, the total flow of capital to the LDCs was $20 billion. Of this, $8.4 billion was private investment, and the remaining $11.8 billion was bilateral and multilateral assistance. If prices of the ten core commodities were doubled, the additional revenue would be about 160 percent of the level of development assistance. To the extent that the price increases would act as a substitute for foreign aid, the net increase in funds available to the LDCs would be smaller. The comparison with OPEC is even less favorable. In 1974, 1975, and 1976, the higher prices enforced by OPEC increased the oil producers' revenues by approximately $80 billion, the bulk of which went to Middle Eastern nations with a total population of less than 100 million.

Table 4-2
Net Revenue Flows to LDCs Through Increased Commodity Prices
(Millions of Dollars)

Commodity	*Percent of Commodity Exported by LDCs*	*Total Increase in Revenue to LDCs*		*Percent of Commodity Imported by LDCs*	*Increase in Cost to LDCs*		*Net Revenue to LDCs*	
		20% Price Increase	*100% Price Increase*		*20% Price Increase*	*100% Price Increase*	*20% Price Increase*	*100% Price Increase*
Cocoa	99.2	387	1,933	3.0	12	58	375	1,874
Coffee	96.8	501	2,507	4.1	21	106	480	2,401
Tea	82.8	119	597	28.6	41	206	78	391
Sugar	69.7	2,123	10,616	22.0	679	3,397	1,444	7,220
Cotton	57.9	504	2,518	16.7	145	726	358	1,792
Jute	95.6	23	113	32.8	8	39	15	74
Sisal	97.7	25	123	5.2	1	7	23	116
Rubber	97.7	170	849	9.6	17	83	153	767
Copper	54.5	831	4,157	7.2	110	549	722	3,607
Tin	85.5	161	804	5.8	11	55	150	749
Bananas	93.3	31	154	6.4	2	11	29	143
Iron ore	37.9	211	1,054	0.8	5	22	206	1,032

Sources: U.N. Food and Agriculture Organization, *Trade Yearbook* (1974), and International Bank for Reconstruction and Development, *Commodity Trade and Price Trends* (1975), and table 4-1.

Table 4-3
Flow of Financial Resources from Developed Countries and Multilateral Agencies to LDCs, 1972
(Billions of Dollars)

Bilateral Assistance		6.8
Grants and grantlike flows	4.4	
Loans at concessional terms	2.4	
Multilateral assistance		4.0
International Bank for Reconstruction and Development	1.9	
Other	2.1	
Grants by voluntary agencies		1.0
Private flows		8.4
Total		20.2

Source: Organization for Economic Cooperation and Development, report by the chairman of the Development Assistance Committee *Development Co-operation, 1974 Review* (Paris: OECD, 1974), pp. 232, 233.

The Historical Record

The estimates that have been presented assume that restrictive commodity agreements would be successful, but a glance at the historical record is enough to create doubts about their prospects. Figure 4-1 shows the periods during which the major international commodity agreements operated.[3] Not all of these agreements attempted to maintain price above the long-run competitive level. Their common features are, with some exceptions noted below, use of restrictions on supply and, sometimes after modest success, failure.

Prewar Agreements

The 1930s were the heyday of commodity agreements, but commodity agreements were not, as figure 4-1 might suggest, an invention of that period. These agreements had evolved from regulatory schemes undertaken in the 1920s by individual governments or groups of private firms. The International Tin Control, for example, was preceded by the Tin Producers Association, and the International Copper Control was preceded by the Copper Exporters Association and Copper Exporters, Incorporated.[4]

The arrangements set up by private firms were generally unsuccessful, and few lasted for long.[5] Although the pattern of failure varied from one case to the next, the dominant theme was the inability of private firms to restrict exports. It

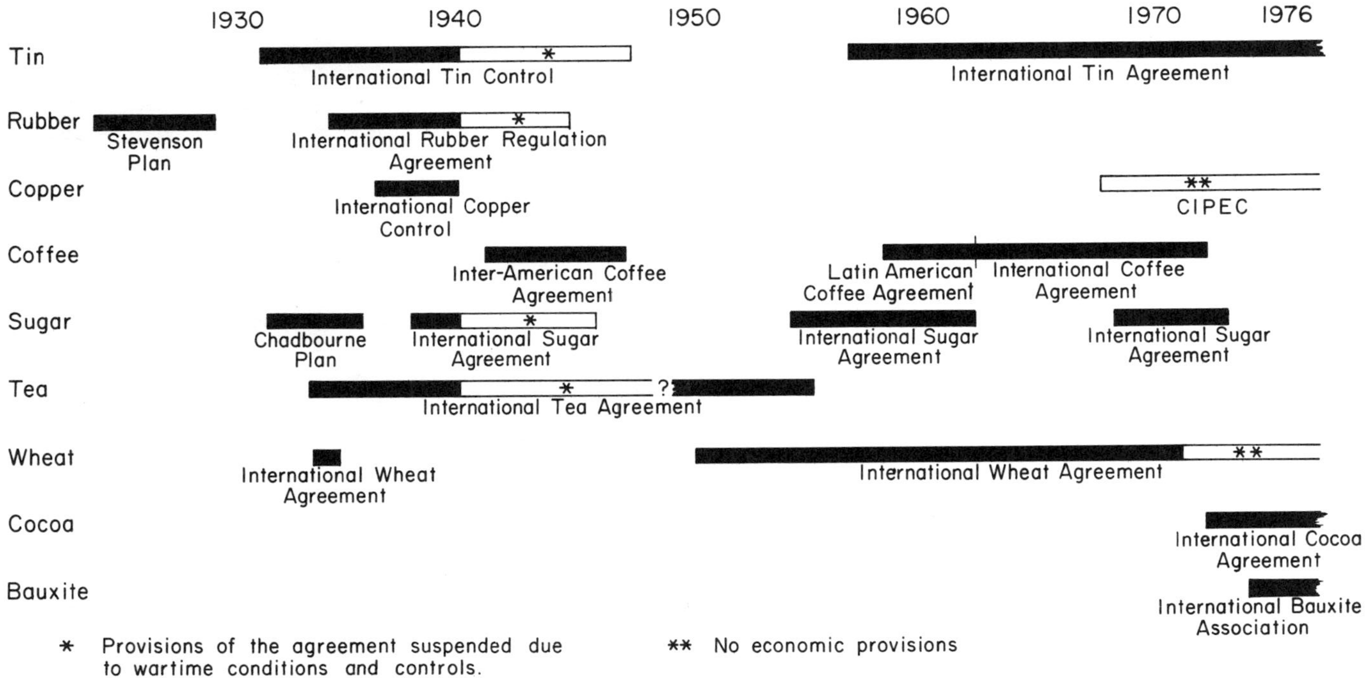

Sources: J. Rowe, *Primary Commodities in International Trade* (Cambridge University Press, 1965); G. Stocking and M. Watkins, *Cartels in Action* (The Twentieth Century Fund, 1947); J. Davis, "Experience Under Intergovernmental Commodity Agreements, 1902-1945," *Journal of Political Economy* 54 (June 1946); U.S. Senate, Committee on Finance, *International Commodity Agreements* (Washington: GPO, 1975); A. Law, *International Commodity Agreements* (Lexington Books, 1975).

Figure 4-1. Major Commodity Agreements

became clear that export quotas could be successfully imposed only by governments, and private schemes gave way to governmental arrangements.

The fate of the Stevenson Plan, however, makes it clear that government involvement is not in itself a guarantee of success. The Stevenson Plan covered rubber production in three British dependencies: Ceylon, the Federated Malay States, and the Straits Settlements. When the plan was inaugurated in 1922, these British colonies produced about 70 percent of the world rubber supply.[6] Rubber prices were increased by the export restrictions imposed by the Stevenson Plan, but therein lay the seeds of the plan's failure. The higher price for natural rubber stimulated the development of synthetic rubber and the increased use of reclaimed rubber. Furthermore, production not covered by the agreement, especially in the Netherlands East Indies, increased dramatically. In 1922, the Dutch accounted for 23.2 percent of world production. By 1927, the year before the Stevenson Plan was abandoned, the Dutch share of the market had increased to 37.7 percent, and the British share had fallen to 54.1 percent.[7]

Profits of rubber growers in the British dependencies were undoubtedly increased for a time by the restrictions on exports imposed by the Stevenson Plan. But expansion of production in areas not covered by the plan eventually reduced the British growers' share of the market without any compensating gain in price. The lesson is that raising prices above the competitive level stimulates expansion of output from competing sources, which eventually breaks the arrangement.

The Chadbourne Plan, which began in May 1931, is another example of the force of increased production.[8] The principal aim of the plan was to work off large stocks of sugar that had accumulated without depressing price. The plan included a schedule for disposal of the stock and bound the participants–Cuba, Java, Peru, and the major European sugar producers–to export quotas. The plan did not succeed in increasing the price of sugar. Although its members reduced their output by about six million tons, the increased supply from nonmembers made up about two-thirds of the reduction.[9] This increase was not a response to higher prices but was instead the "result of the intensified programs of numerous consuming countries for fostering domestic production."[10] Nevertheless, the increase in sugar production by nonmembers limited the profitability of the Chadbourne Plan, and it was not renewed when the agreement expired in 1935.

The International Sugar Agreement of 1937 responded to the Chadbourne Plan's failures. The Stevenson Plan was also, in this respect, the predecessor of the International Rubber Regulation Agreement of 1934. There is a more general sense in which the commodity agreements of the late 1930s were successors of earlier failures. Commentators on this period suggest that past experience had taught three lessons. First, unilateral schemes, or agreements among private firms, did not work, which implies that restrictive arrangements must be based on agreements among governments. Apart from any role that political means may have in gaining the necessary coverage for an agreement, governments have the means of enforcing export quotas. Second, to have a chance of success an agreement must include very nearly all suppliers. Third, to be successful, an agreement must behave in a moderate way; in particular, it must not attempt to increase price above the long-run competitive level.[11]

The agreements in effect at the start of World War II—those for copper, rubber, sugar, tea, and tin—generally honored these lessons, and they at least avoided collapse. Although the International Rubber Regulation Agreement was shaky and might have failed in any event, each of these agreements effectively ended only with the imposition of wartime controls.

Avoidance of collapse, of course, is a rather minimal achievement. If OPEC's quadrupling of the price of oil is taken as a standard, then none of these agreements was a success; in fact, by this test, all previous commodity agreements have been failures. But there is a consensus that, in more limited terms, the commodity agreements of the mid to late 1930s were reasonably successful.

The nature and extent of their success reflects the special circumstances of the 1930s. From 1930 to the start of World War II, the commodity markets were, with scattered exceptions and interruptions, severely depressed. In these circumstances, commodity prices fall to the level of average variable cost of production. Marginal suppliers are driven from the market, and all producers fail to cover capital costs. This situation continues until, by the elimination of suppliers, the size of the industry has been accommodated to the drastically reduced level of demand.

The five commodity agreements that persisted to World War II were a response to such a situation. Their means were monopolistic, as was their aim—to increase prices—but it seems that most of these agreements attempted only to increase price to long-run average cost. The incentive for overshipping would remain, but given that price was not increased above the long-run average cost of efficient operations, the viability of the agreement would not be challenged by entry. By a combination of different circumstances and moderate behavior, then, the commodity agreements of the 1930s avoided a principal cause of the failure of earlier restrictive schemes. Their major purpose was apparently to preserve existing suppliers pending a recovery of demand, and in this respect they were reasonably successful.

The Postwar Agreements

The postwar agreements differ from those of the 1930s in that importing nations were more often included. The exceptions to this rule are the Latin-American Coffee Agreement, the International Tea Agreement, the International Bauxite Association, and Conseil International des Pays Exportateurs du Cuivre (CIPEC), all of which include only exporting nations. But, like the agreements of the

1930s, those of the postwar period have relied primarily on export controls.[12]

Altogether ten commodity agreements have operated at some time since World War II. The International Tin Agreement has been moderately successful, and CIPEC, the International Bauxite Association, and the International Cocoa Agreement still exist. The other six agreements must be counted as failures in the straightforward sense that they broke down or were not renewed with economic provisions.

By far, the most frequent cause of failure among postwar agreements was disputes between importing and exporting nations over price ranges and/or export quotas. This was the principal factor in the failure of the second International Sugar Agreement,[13] the International Wheat Agreement,[14] and the International Coffee Agreement.[15] A dispute between coffee suppliers and the United States over prices may also provide part of the explanation for the dropping of export quotas from the Inter-American Coffee Agreement in 1946.[16]

The other three postwar failures do not fall into any simple pattern. It is not entirely clear why the International Tea Agreement (ITA) was not renewed in 1955. The ITA was, in any event, a very mild arrangement and perhaps was not continued because it accomplished very little.[17] The first International Sugar Agreement was brought down by a dispute between Cuba and other suppliers over market shares.[18] Finally, the failure of the Latin American Coffee Agreement (LACA) echoes earlier experience. In 1962, after four years of operation, the LACA was on the brink of suffering the fate of the Stevenson and Chadbourne plans, and for essentially the same reasons. The price of coffee had declined over the life of the agreement and in 1962 Brazil's carry-over stock exceeded total world coffee exports of the preceding year.[19] This situation was retrieved when the United States indicated its willingness to join a coffee agreement, and the LACA was replaced by the International Coffee Agreement.[20] Thus, although the LACA did not literally collapse, it must be considered a failure.

The postwar record of commodity agreements as a whole confirmed one aspect of the experience with commodity agreements during the 1920s and 1930s: such arrangements are not very successful in raising prices. Some of the postwar agreements had brief success in this respect. For example, "The 1964 price jump (to nearly 50¢) must be considered the direct result of the coffee agreement, with only minor, if any, assistance from the weather."[21] The International Tin Agreement, to give another example, enjoyed its customary success in limiting declines in price. There were not, however, any dramatic successes.

Structural Sources of Instability

Although a comparative analysis seems indicated by the successes and failures, it cannot be done because, apart from the tin agreements, there are no clear examples of success. The analysis would come down to a search for special features of the tin agreements, which does not appear to be a very promising line. Given the nature of the historical record, it seems better to look into the sources of failure.

Ten of the eighteen agreements can be labeled failures. The distribution of the principal causes of failure, for the eight cases in which a cause can be designated, is as follows: disputes among sellers over market share, 1; overshipping, 1; entry, 3; and disputes between importing and exporting nations, 3. It is not entirely clear why the International Tea Agreement and the Inter-American Coffee Agreement failed. Five of the eight remaining agreements ended with World War II, and four are currently in existence.

The Tractable Problems

Neither overshipping nor disputes among participants over market shares were important causes of failure of past agreements, and they might be dismissed from further discussion with that observation. However, there is something to be learned by looking at why disputes over market shares and overshipping have not usually been fatal problems.

Disputes over market shares are not uncommon, and they certainly can lead to the failure of an agreement. The most difficult problems would be posed by a recent, low-cost entrant. Such a supplier would probably begin with a small share of the market but insist on a larger share and threaten to withdraw if its demands were not satisfied. The threat could be potentially dangerous because a low-cost supplier might be able to do better outside the agreement than by accepting a relatively small market share within the agreement. If demand is growing, the other suppliers may be able to satisfy the demands of the low cost producer without reducing their output. But if demand is not growing, or not growing rapidly enough, the other producers can meet the low-cost supplier's demand for an increased market share only by moving over.

The prewar tin agreements provide an instructive example of the successful resolution of a problem of this sort. The tin agreement, concluded in 1933, was first extended for one year. Negotiations on renewal of the agreement in 1936 encountered serious difficulties when Thailand and what was then the Belgian Congo insisted on larger market shares. In the resulting impasse, Britain and Portugal temporarily withdrew from the talks. The nature of the solution is indicated by the data in table 4-4. The large producers–Bolivia, British Malaya, and the Netherlands East Indies–gave up part of their shares of the market in favor of Thailand and the Belgian Congo.[22]

The failure of the first postwar International Sugar Agreement in 1961 provides the only example in which a dispute among suppliers over market share led to the failure of a major commodity agreement, and this is a rather special case. In 1960, the United States embargoed sugar imports from Cuba. Cuba, while making large sales to the U.S.S.R., attempted to negotiate increased quotas with other Western nations to replace sales to the United States, thus maintaining its share of the noncommunist market. This solution was unacceptable to other suppliers, and the agreement broke down.[23]

The reason why disputes over market shares have seldom led to the failure of agreements grows out of the logic of profit maximization. Suppose, for the sake of simplicity, that all producers have the same costs. In this case, it is clear that there is some total output and a corresponding price that maximizes the profits of suppliers as a group. If an agreement is not reached and output is not restricted, price and total profits will be less than maximal. Consequently, there is some distribution of market shares that leaves every producer better off than it would be in the absence of an agreement. The negotiating problem is to find such a satisfactory distribution of market shares. It would be virtually impossible to do so if there are a very large number of suppliers in the industry, but for most of the commodity industries, negotiation of market shares is a practical possibility.

Overshipping, like disputes over market shares, is common. It was a major problem for the International Coffee Agreement in the mid-1960s and, forty years earlier, for the Stevenson Plan.[24] The difficulty in the latter case was not that participating governments cheated but rather that individual producers smuggled rubber out of the country.[25] These cases are simple examples; to a greater or lesser extent, overshipping afflicted virtually all past agreements. However, it seems to have been a principal cause of failure only of the first International Wheat Agreement. Argentina had a bumper wheat crop in 1933-1934 and exceeded its quota to a noticeable extent. This and a related dispute over limitations on production brought the IWA down.[26] In general, it seems that overshipping was prevalent but usually held to tolerable levels.

The structure of suppliers' incentives does not provide a clear-cut rational-

Table 4-4
Standard Tonnages under the Second and Third International Tin Control Agreements (Percent of Total)

Country	*Second Agreement*	*Third Agreement*
British Malaya	38.1	36.0
Netherlands East Indies	19.2	18.2
Thailand	7.0	9.0
French Indochina	1.7	1.5
Belgian Congo	3.6	6.6
Nigeria	5.8	5.4
Bolivia	24.6	23.3

Source: K. Knorr, *Tin under Control* (Stanford, 1945), p. 152.

ization of this fact. On the one hand, the ancient insight that producers can increase their profit by colluding to limit supply is valid and important. Overshipping by any one producer can lead to overshipping by others, and hence to the collapse of the agreement and lower profits for all. On the other hand, cheating can appear to be profitable to an individual supplier. Given that a price above incremental cost has been established, any supplier can increase profits by overshipping so long as the practice does not become general.

The balance of these two forces can be such that suppliers restrain themselves from overshipping. Whether a restrictive agreement would have this feature depends primarily on the degree to which supply is concentrated. In particular, if no small group of sellers retains a preponderant share of the market, significant overshipping is more likely to occur as the number of suppliers increases.

How few sellers is few enough for a restrictive agreement to be self-policing is a matter of informed judgment. Most students of industrial behavior would agree that collusive arrangements tend to be stable in industries dominated by three or four sellers, and many would extend this to industries with eight to ten major suppliers. These judgments, however, primarily reflect domestic experience, and international restrictive arrangements would probably be more prone to instability with any given number of sellers.[27] Unfortunately, it is not clear how much more stringent a test should be applied in judging international agreements.

Table 4-5 shows the share of the four largest suppliers among the LDCs in each of seventeen commodities. The four largest suppliers hold at least 75 percent of the export markets in six of these commodities (cocoa, jute, rubber, sisal, tea, and tin). The figures for jute, sisal, and rubber, however, may be

Table 4-5
Export Market Shares of the Four Largest LDC Producers, Average, 1970-1972 (Percent)

Cocoa	74.5	Tin	75.3
Coffee	54.4	Bananas	57.4
Tea	66.3	Bauxite	59.9
Sugar	42.5	Iron ore	25.9
Cotton	30.8	Beef	23.9
Jute	94.2	Wheat	3.3
Sisal	80.7	Rice	26.2
Rubber	87.6	Wool	9.4
Copper	47.7		

Source: International Bank for Reconstruction and Development, *Commodity Trade and Price Trends* (1975).

misleading because each of these commodities faces strong competition from synthetic products. If the markets were defined as including the synthetic substitutes, concentration in rubber, jute, and sisal would be low. But concentration in the export markets for cocoa, tea, and tin is high enough to suggest that suppliers would behave cooperatively. The extent of concentration in the export markets for bananas, bauxite, coffee, and copper falls into an ambiguous range, and concentration in the export markets for the remaining seven commodities is low.[28]

It seems that the degree of concentration in the commodity industries, or by implication, the strength of suppliers' incentives to cheat, would not always provide a cogent explanation of why overshipping was not a fatal problem. Another, and simpler, possibility is that commodity agreements had adequate means to cope with the problem.

Some past agreements have established free zones in which members and nonmembers can supply as much as they choose.[29] The price in the free zone is determined by the play of the market and, presumably, would always be less than the controlled price. Its existence creates a strong incentive for purchasers in the free zone to resell in the regulated zone, so the arrangement is viable only if the two zones are separated from one another by high transport costs, selective tariffs, or legal barriers. Furthermore, a free zone does not eliminate the producers' incentive to overship to the controlled zone; it only somewhat reduces the temptation to do so. The establishment of a free zone, then, is not a very effective way of dealing with the problem of overshipping.

The second, and potentially much more effective, mechanism, is a certificate system, which transfers the problem of enforcing export quotas to importers.[30] The ICO would create certificates, denominated in physical units, and allocate to each supplier the certificates required to cover its quota. Importing nations would agree to reject shipments that were not accompanied by the appropriate certificates. A certificate system involves some administrative problems. For example, there is a question of what to do about imports to country A via country B and delays in transit. A certificate system also sets up incentives for counterfeiting and smuggling. But since these problems are within the reach of importing nations' customs services, there is not much doubt that a certificate system could be reasonably effective.

The thrust of these comments is that neither disputes over market shares nor overshipping are critical problems, but for different reasons. Disputes over market shares are held in check by suppliers' incentives, so no institutional means of solving such disputes as arise is required. The incentives that work on suppliers are such that overshipping can be expected and could destroy an agreement if left unchecked. But overshipping is a problem for which there are solutions.

The Intractable Problems

Disputes between buyers and sellers and entry are problems to which the mechanisms available to commodity agreements provide no ready solution. It is thus not surprising to find that disputes between buyers and sellers and entry account for six of the eight clear failures in the historical record.

There is no difficulty in recognizing the source of disputes between importing and exporting nations: within a restrictive arrangement, their immediate economic interests are opposed. Suppliers have (up to a point) an interest in higher prices, while it is in the importers' interest to resist restrictions of supply and higher prices. Importers do have a long-term interest in continuity of supply, but this interest is by and large served by the market and is apt to look nebulous in the face of the prospect of significant increases in price. Importing nations, in short, are not attracted to restrictive arrangements by their immediate economic interests. Nor is it reasonable to suppose that importers are forced into restrictive arrangements by suppliers; if suppliers had the requisite power, they presumably would use it as the OPEC nations did. A discussion of the role that importers play in restrictive arrangements and the question of why they would ever participate is, however, postponed to the following chapter. For the moment, the point is that suppliers' and buyers' immediate interests are opposed in a restrictive arrangement, and commodity agreements contain no means of enforcing a reconciliation of this conflict.

The difficulty of entry, and as the extent to which entry is potentially a problem, differs somewhat between the metals industries and the agricultural industries. Relatively large capital costs are an impediment to entry into the metals industries. Entry into metals mining, furthermore, requires finding an ore body that can be exploited profitably. Such discoveries are made from time to time, but they are not routine occurrences. Although detailed study might suggest otherwise, there is a presumption that entry into the metals industries is difficult. This does not mean that it is impossible. A significant price increase would spur efforts to find new deposits and hasten the development of deposits already known, and over the course of a decade these forces probably would call forth a few new suppliers. Entry into the agricultural industries, in contrast, is much easier and could be expected to occur more rapidly. Some agricultural commodities require relatively specialized conditions for their cultivation, but even within these limitations, the scope for entry is substantial. In some cases, significant price increases would attract entrants within a year or two. Cocoa, coffee, rubber, and tea are exceptions to this rule. Although price increases would encourage additional plantings, the trees (or bushes) require several years to mature and begin yielding regular crops; thus, the effects would not be felt immediately.

Within these structural conditions, the extent to which a restrictive agreement will attract entry depends on how supply restrictions are employed. If supply is restricted only temporarily, and only in periods when demand is low relative to existing production capability, significant entry may not be attracted, although even in this case, the higher average price promised by the use of export controls may attract some new suppliers to the market. But an incentive for entry is definitely set up if export quotas are used on a more or less permanent basis to increase price. To say that price is above the long-run competitive equilibrium means that returns in the industry are relatively high, and potential suppliers can be expected to cash in on such a situation.

Entrants could be admitted to the arrangement, which might permit total supply to be restricted enough to maintain price above the competitive level. However, members of the arrangement would have to move over to accommodate entrants, and their profits would at least be drastically reduced. In fact, reductions in output are likely to increase costs to the extent that no member of the arrangement earns more than the competitive rate of return.[31] Consequently, admitting entrants to the arrangement does not solve the problem of entry, and as the fate of the Stevenson and Chadbourne plans illustrates, a restrictive arrangement will eventually collapse under such pressures.

The only alternative to unimpeded entry and admitting entrants is an attempt to exclude entrants or at least drastically limit the amount of entry. A strong certificate system, coupled perhaps with a free zone, could succeed. However, it is difficult to see why importing nations should agree to enforce certificate systems, and attempts to limit entry would be at the very least highly contentious. What is involved is exclusion, by an international agency, of efforts by individual nations to create and expand particular industries. Entry, like disputes between buyers and sellers, is thus a problem without a clear solution.

Concluding Comments

It would not be correct to conclude on the basis of the evidence presented here that restrictive commodity arrangements simply do not work. First, although its objectives seem quite modest, the tin agreement has been successful for many years and, except for the International Rubber Regulation, the agreements of the 1930s seem to have been brought down by World War II rather than by economic forces. Second, some restrictive arrangements have worked for brief periods and, while they maintained high prices, profited suppliers. Finally, it is possible to conceive of means that would succeed in stabilizing restrictive agreements.

Nevertheless, the problems faced by restrictive arrangements are formidable. Most of the agreements reviewed in this chapter were not intended to produce dramatic, permanent increases in price. Their aims in most cases were the more moderate ones of preventing steep declines in price and maintaining the average price at what is often called a fair level. The very limited success that such arrangements have had is a testament to the power of the economic forces set up whenever price is increased even moderately above the competitive level.

Notes

1. The International Cocoa Agreement makes provision for a buffer stock, but, because the market price has been far above the floor price since the agreement went into effect in 1970, the cocoa buffer stock has not operated.

2. For example, the long-run elasticity of demand for copper is more than twice the short-run elasticity. See F. Fisher, P. Cootner, and N. Baily, "An Econometric Model of the World Copper Industry," *Bell Journal of Economics* 3 (Autumn 1972):568-609. Some commodities–especially sisal and jute–face strong competition from synthetic products. A significant increase in the prices of these commodities is virtually precluded by competition.

3. This figure excludes all nongovernment and unilateral schemes, informal arrangements under the U.N. Food and Agriculture Organization, and some very specialized agreements.

4. See J.W.F. Rowe, *Primary Commodities in International Trade* (Cambridge: Cambridge University Press, 1965), chap. 10, esp. pp. 125-126, and chap. 12, pp. 140-143.

5. Discussions of various private control schemes can be found in Rudolf K. Michels, *Cartels, Combines and Trusts in Post-War Germany* (New York: Columbia University Press, 1928), Alfred Plummer, *International Combines in Modern Industry* (London: Sir Isaac Pitman and Sons, 1938), George W. Stocking and Myron W. Watkins, *Cartels in Action* (New York: The Twentieth Century Fund, 1947), and Benjamin B. Wallace and Lynn R. Edminster, *International Control of Raw Materials* (Washington, D.C.: The Brookings Institution, 1930).

6. Stocking and Watkins, *Cartels in Action*, pp. 65-66.

7. Ibid., p. 72. The British share increased to about 66 percent in 1929.

8. The Chadbourne Plan was an agreement among the sugar-producer associations, but the governments of the nations concerned agreed to pass the legislation necessary to enforce export quotas and, with one unimportant exception, did so. See ibid., p. 66.

9. Rowe, *Primary Commodities*, pp. 146-147.

10. Stocking and Watkins, *Cartels in Action*, p. 41.

11. This is an interpretation of statements made by Joseph S. Davis, "Experience Under Intergovernmental Commodity Agreements, 1902-1945," *Journal of Political Economy* 54 (1946):193-220, and especially Rowe, *Primary Commodities*, chap. 12. The generality is not, of course, equally true of all of the agreements of the 1930s.

12. The principal exceptions are the International Wheat Agreement, which was a multilateral purchase and sale commitment, and the International Bauxite

Association, whose members have individually imposed taxes on bauxite. CIPEC was formed without economic provisions, although it attempted to limit its members' exports in 1973 and 1974. The International Tin Agreement and the International Cocoa Agreement provide for buffer stocks, although the cocoa buffer stock has not yet operated.

13. U.S., Congress, *Report by Congressional Advisors to UNCTAD IV* (Washington, D.C.: Government Printing Office, 1976), pp. 132-133.

14. Ibid., p. 118. See also Vernon L. Sorenson, *International Trade Policy: Agriculture and Development* (East Lansing: Division of Research, Graduate School of Business Administration, Michigan State University, 1975), pp. 163-164, and, for a discussion of the postwar history of wheat agreements, Rowe, *Primary Commodities*, pp. 163-169.

15. Alton D. Law, *International Commodity Agreements* (Lexington, Mass.: Lexington Books, 1975), p. 45.

16. Rowe, *Primary Commodities*, p. 178.

17. Davis, "Experience Under Intergovernmental Commodity Agreements," pp. 199-202.

18. Rowe, *Primary Commodities*, p. 177.

19. Ibid., p. 179.

20. Ibid., pp. 179-180.

21. Law, *International Commodity Agreements*, p. 44.

22. See Irving Kravis, "International Commodity Agreements to Promote Aid and Efficiency: The Case of Coffee," *Canadian Journal of Economics* 1 (1968), esp. 298, for a description of a similar situation in coffee.

23. Rowe, *Primary Commodities*, p. 177.

24. Kravis, "International Commodity Agreements," pp. 295-317, esp. p. 305.

25. Stocking and Watkins, *Cartels in Action*, pp. 74-76.

26. Davis, "Experience Under Intergovernmental Commodity Agreements," p. 205.

27. This would be true in part simply because of the greater difficulty of communication across national boundaries. The more important reason has to do with the fact that international arrangements would rely on restrictions on supply to maintain price rather than on direct agreement on price. Overshipping is more difficult to detect than price cutting and hence can be expected to be more prevalent.

28. However, only about one-third of noncommunist world copper is produced in the LDCs.

29. A free zone has been used in postwar coffee agreements. See G.D. Gwyer, "Three International Commodity Agreements: The Experience of East Africa," *Economic Development and Cultural Change* 21 (October 1972):306, and Davis, "Experience Under Intergovernmental Commodity Agreements," p. 207.

30. Certificate systems were used in the International Coffee Agreement and the Inter-American Coffee Agreement. See Kravis, "International Commodity Agreements," p. 306 and Davis, "Experience Under Intergovernmental Commodity Agreements," p. 207.

31. See Don Patinkin, "Multi-plant Firms, Cartels, and Imperfect Competition," *Quarterly Journal of Economics* 61 (February 1947):173-205, and Dean A. Worchester, Jr., "Why 'Dominant' Firms Decline," *Journal of Political Economy* 65 (1957):338-346.

5 Integrated Commodity Programs

The similarities among the commodity markets are enough to lead attention from agreements for individual products to the possibility of a system of arrangements covering major commodities. From the LDCs' point of view, this is an obvious step for both economic and political reasons. But this idea is only a point of departure, and it carries no implications for either the type of agreement or for the ways in which agreements could be related. At one extreme, individual agreements might disappear as separate legal entities to become programs within an international organization. At the other extreme, individual agreements might be related only by a highly specialized and limited financial institution. There are many possibilities between these two and many ways of accommodating different types of commodity agreements within an umbrella organization.

The Integrated Programme for Commodities (IPC), although not the only example of a plan for a related set of commodity agreements, is the best developed of the proposals that have been made and thus provides a useful basis for discussion. It is necessary to add that the documents describing the IPC are silent on some important topics, unclear on others, and occasionally take contradictory positions. These lacunae will be of principal interest in what follows because they point toward the range of possibilities inherent in notion of an integrated program.

Provisions of the Integrated Programme for Commodities

The various parts of the IPC are not integrated in any formal way. The individual international commodity organizations (ICOs) would be legally separate from the Common Fund, which would not exercise any managerial control over them. The Common Fund would not even have the policy review function that Keynes assigned his General Council on Commodity Controls. Altogether the IPC is more a collection of components than a system.

The Common Fund is conceived of as essentially a financial institution. Its initial capital would be contributed by member nations, and additional funds would be raised by borrowing. Reports by the UNCTAD Secretariat suggest an initial contribution of $1 billion and borrowings of $2 billion, which could be followed by an additional contribution of $1 billion and additional borrowing of $2 billion, for an eventual total capital of $6 billion.[1]

This sum would be divided into two administratively separate funds, one of which would make loans to ICOs to finance buffer stocks.[2] These loans are intended to be lines of credit, which the ICOs would draw on when making purchases and then would repay when the stock is sold. UNCTAD documents suggest that $5 billion be devoted to loans to ICOs for buffer stocks.[3] The Common Fund's remaining $1 billion would go into a fund that would make loans for diversification programs—research and development, market promotion, and investment projects of various sorts. These loans might be made directly to individual countries, but they would normally be made to ICOs, which would then relend the funds to their members.[4]

The Common Fund is not intended to carry on managerial functions, but there is one respect in which it would go beyond a strictly financial role. In emergency situations, it could, subject to certain restrictions, trade in a commodity on its own account. To do so, it would be necessary to have the approval of suppliers representing 50 percent of total supply and a qualified majority of the executive board.[5]

The policy-making apparatus of the Common Fund would be similar to that employed by existing international financial institutions. Policy would be made through a board of governors, on which all member nations would be represented, and a much smaller executive board.[6] The documents on the Common Fund make no suggestions on the distribution of powers between the board of governors and executive board or on the allocation of votes, an issue of obvious importance.[7] If votes are allocated primarily in terms of capital subscriptions, the DCs would control the Common Fund; under other formulas (such as one country, one vote), control would be in the hands of the LDCs.

The character of the Common Fund creates a presumption that the individual ICOs would be buffer stocks, and the IPC does envision the creation of buffer stocks but not pure buffer stocks. Table 5-1 lists the economic measures suggested for each of sixteen commodities in a report by the UNCTAD Secretariat. Buffer stocks are proposed for all of the commodities except bananas, for which a buffer stock arrangement is clearly infeasible, bauxite, and iron ore. Storage problems rule out a buffer stock for iron ore, and the prevalence of intracompany transfers, along with some other factors, seems to rule out a buffer stock for bauxite.[8] Pure buffer stocks (those without supply management) are suggested for tea, cotton, and, perhaps, wool. In the other ten (counting wool, eleven) cases, the buffer stocks would be coupled with supply management measures.

A buffer stock and multilateral purchase and sales commitment (MPSC) were suggested for wheat and rice, which were excluded from the IPC in resolution 93 (IV) adopted at UNCTAD IV, and sugar. In the remaining eight cases, the buffer stock would be supported by export and/or production controls and, in some cases, multilateral purchase and sales commitment as well. Each of these eight commodities, except wool, is in the core group, on which an IPC would be initially based.

Table 5-1
Economic Measures for Sixteen Commodities Suggested in UNCTAD TD/B/C.1/194

Commodity	*Buffer Stock*	*Supply Management*	*Certificate System*
Cocoa	√	Export quotas	
Coffee	√	Export quotas	√
Tea	√		
Sugar	√	MPSC	
Bananas		Export quotas and MPSC	
Wheat	√	MPSC	
Rice	√	MPSC	
Cotton	√		
Rubber	√	Export quotas and MPSC	√[a]
Jute	√	Export and production controls	
Wool	√	Export quotas (?)	
Hard fibers	√	Export and production controls	
Copper	√	Export quotas and MPSC	
Iron ore		MPSC	
Tin	√	Export quotas and MPSC	
Bauxite		MPSC	

Source: U.N. Conference on Trade and Development, Trade and Development Board, "An Integrated Programme for Commodities: Measures for Individual Commodities," TD/B/C.1/194, October 1, 1975.

[a]UNCTAD, TD/B/IPC/RUBBER/L.2, para. 46, p. 14.

UNCTAD documents envision a permanent use of export quotas and/or production controls in some cases. Supply management measures are then described as a way of balancing supply and demand over the long run; for example,

> . . . it is believed that commodity arrangements should secure the maintenance of a reasonable relationship over time with the products exchanged for them in international trade. Measures to this end would therefore be based on the proposition that, where feasible, the supply of commodities should be managed to bring supply into equilibrium with demand at desired price trends.[9]

The desired price would clearly be above the long-run competitive price, since at the latter, the quantity that producers are willing to supply equals the quantity that buyers are willing to purchase. Most of the ICOs described by UNCTAD, however, do not fall into this clear-cut case. For one commodity (copper), restrictions on supply are to be used on a strictly temporary basis in emergency situations.[10] In the remaining cases, UNCTAD reports leave open the question of whether restrictions on supply are to be used on a temporary or permanent basis.

UNCTAD reports suggest certificate systems for coffee[11] and rubber[12] and state that a method of policing production controls for jute would probably not be necessary.[13] In other cases, although the use of controls on supply is suggested, no mention is made of enforcement mechanisms.

In addition to buffer stocks and/or supply management, UNCTAD Secretariat reports suggest that each ICO create a diversification fund, which would be built up through contributions by suppliers or a tax on the commodity, loans from the Common Fund, and, perhaps, contributions by importers. Loans or grants would be made to countries to enable them to shift resources from the commodity covered by the ICO to other industries.[14] Presumably, this would be a way of curing chronic oversupply, although whether there is such an oversupply depends on a good deal on the level of price.

Various UNCTAD documents discuss other aspects of the IPC's commodity agreements—voting procedures, contributions, determination of price ranges and so on. These topics will be mentioned below, but, for the moment, the main point is simply that, with few exceptions, the arrangements suggested by the UNCTAD Secretariat are far from being pure buffer stocks.

Operation of the IPC

It is often taken for granted that the IPC would increase the prices of the commodities included above the competitive level. Although this may well be the intent, the IPC is not simply a straightforward set of cartel-like arrangements. Some elements of the IPC go toward price raising, some toward reducing price fluctuations, and the role of others is not immediately obvious. In addition, the management of the Common Fund and the individual ICOs involves an element of discretion. In short, the IPC possesses a complicated problem of diagnosis.

Discussions of the IPC have centered on the Common Fund. This emphasis is appropriate, but to appreciate the roles that a Common Fund might play, it is necessary first to look into the operation of the commodity agreements envisioned by the IPC.

The IPC's Commodity Agreements

An UNCTAD report published in 1968 concluded that buffer stocks that used supply management on only a supplementary basis would avoid many of the problems that afflicted past agreements that relied on controls over supply.[15] This may be so, but any ICO, simply as an organization, provides a focus for suppliers' interest in higher prices, and for this reason alone, there is a question as to whether buffer stocks would tend to degenerate into restrictive schemes.

Keynes held that only experience could provide an answer, but he built several strong safeguards into his proposal.[16] The question is more forceful for the IPC because it lacks these safeguards.

A buffer stock with provisions for supply management can be led into difficulties by flaws in its operating rules. If the target price of a buffer stock is set above the competitive level, additional supply from existing producers will be encouraged in the short run; and, over the long run, entrants will be attracted, and/or existing producers will be induced to expand their capacity. If too high a target price is set, the buffer stock creates a situation of excess supply. Maintaining the target price by purchases would be expensive and would lead to an ever-increasing stock. But if purchases are discontinued, price must fall, and suppliers will be driven from the market. Faced with these prospects, an ICO will be very apt to decide that restrictions on supply are the appropriate response.

This scenario grows out of the assumption that the target price is set above the long-run competitive level. If it is maintained at the long-run competitive level, new capacity will not be created, and a stock will not be endlessly accumulated. How the target price is adjusted is, then, a crucial consideration.

One possibility is a periodic renegotiation of the target price. The rules of the ICO could state that the negotiations are to be on the basis of long-run average cost, but this rule would not be very restrictive. Target price would basically be determined by the bargaining power and positions of importing and exporting nations. The importers' interests would lead them to seek a target price equal to long-run average cost. Exporting nations might recognize that a high price could endanger the existence of the ICO and hence agree to a target price equal to long-run average cost. However, because governments are not often so farsighted, there is a presumption that exporting nations would be led by considerations of short-run gain to seek a price above long-run average cost. The result is likely to be a compromise price greater than long-run average cost but less than the price sought by sellers.

Instead of relying on negotiations, the commodity agreement could specify that target price must equal long-run average cost and delegate the task of estimating this cost to the ICO staff. Given the difficulty of making precise and defensible estimates of cost and the importance of target price to both buyers and sellers, it is unlikely that this approach would be acceptable.

The final possibility is for the members of the ICO to agree on a simple automatic rule. The leading possibilities are: indexation and a moving average of past prices. Under the first of these methods, the target price would be set equal to a base price times an index of the prices paid by the LDCs for imports.[17] Changes in commodity prices would then parallel changes in import prices, but there would be no intelligible relationship between the target price and the competitive price.

The conclusion of chapter 3 that a moving average target price would track the long-run competitive price assumed that supply was not controlled and does not necessarily hold if supply management measures are used in conjunction with a buffer stock. Where a properly designed pure buffer stock would act symmetrically to defend the floor and ceiling prices, a buffer stock with supply management would defend the floor price but would have a limited ability to defend the ceiling price. Hence, even if the target price is set at the competitive level, the use of restrictions on supply to defend the floor price will tend to produce an average price that is above the competitive level. Furthermore, setting the target price for a buffer stock as a moving average of past market prices is meaningless if the market prices are manipulated by controls on supply. This observation takes on a pointed significance in terms of the scenario described above. If a buffer stock begins with a target price that is too high and thereby creates excess supply the use of controls on supply may simply ratify the initial mistake.

Importing nations, or importing and exporting nations, could consciously hold a buffer stock in check, but it is doubtful that they would. Disputes between importing and exporting nations are a leading cause of the failure of commodity agreements. There are substantive safeguards that reduce the likelihood that a buffer stock would degenerate into a restrictive arrangement. However, the agreements sketched in UNCTAD reports do not contain these safeguards, and there is a strong presumption that, in their absence, buffer stocks would tend to become restrictive arrangements and would tend to suffer the same instability that has characterized restrictive arrangements in the past.

Political Economy of a Common Fund

The financial role of the Common Fund is large enough to ensure that it would be involved with any serious problems encountered by an individual ICO. Just as large creditors usually control the policy of a failing business, so the Common Fund would have a significant voice in the affairs of a troubled ICO.

Thought along this line leads to the question of the extent to which the LDCs could use the powers of a Common Fund to stabilize individual ICOs. The Common Fund could respond directly to the problems of entry and oversupply with loans to the ICO for the acquisition of stocks and for diversification, but if only because of limitations on funds available, such steps are unlikely to be more than palliatives. To the extent that the Common Fund could stabilize individual ICOs, the solution must lie elsewhere.

The adherence of importing nations is the key to the problem of stabilizing restrictive arrangements. As a matter of history, disputes between importing and exporting nations were a leading cause of the failure of past agreements. More important, importing nations could enforce a certificate system, which provides a means of limiting entry. If, then, the adherence of importing nations could somehow be guaranteed, the principal causes of the failure of past agreements could be eliminated.

Where an individual ICO will almost invariably be of limited significance to the DCs, the Common Fund would bear much of the burden of the relationship between the DCs and the LDCs. The DCs, then, would be attached to the Common Fund by their broad interest in international stability, as well as a range of lesser concerns, and such an institution would not be lightly abandoned. Adherence to the Common Fund and adherence to individual ICOs are not the same thing, however, and a Common Fund such as that described in UNCTAD reports would not exercise any direct managerial control over the individual ICOs. But it could attack the problem of stabilizing restrictive arrangements to the extent that it could influence the outcome of bargaining within the ICO. The strength of this ability, in turn, would depend on the character of the relations between the Common Fund and the individual ICOs.

Loans for buffer stock activities as well as for diversification could, and very probably would be conditioned on the ICO's providing for the use of export and/or production controls.[18] This requirement could be put as a matter of financial prudence because the possibility of restricting supply is a way of guaranteeing the value of the stock. But, whatever the rationale, the importers' natural position in opposition to restrictions on supply would be undercut because it could be argued (with some cogency) within the ICO that the funds required to make the arrangement effective are available only if a means for regulating supply is created.

Loans for buffer stocks would also tend to involve the Common Fund in the affairs of the ICO in another way. If an ICO fails, its stocks, to the extent that they are financed by loans from the Common Fund, would pass to the Common Fund. The failure of an agreement would then automatically involve the Common Fund in the market. Recognition of this possibility presumably would lead to a more or less direct involvement of the Common Fund in the affairs of a troubled ICO.

The strength of the Common Fund's position in such situations would be increased by its power to trade on its own account in certain situations. The failure of an ICO probably would be regarded as an emergency situation. To trade, the Common Fund would then need the approval of suppliers accounting for one-half of total supply and a qualified majority of its executive board. The requirement of approval might provide importers with a veto power over trading by the fund, but this is by no means certain. The prospect of direct intervention by the Common Fund if an agreement fails might then be used to put pressure on buyers to make concessions necessary to maintain the agreement.

Beyond these specific mechanisms, major issues that arise within ICOs are likely to reach the level of the Common Fund informally and there become elements in a process of logrolling.[19] Because the commitment to establish prices that are fair to buyers and remunerative to producers is open-ended, the DCs would be under pressure to resolve these problems by somehow buying off one or more of the parties to the dispute.

It is thus possible to see the outline of a coherent approach to the problem of stabilizing ICOs. The Common Fund would mobilize and focus the economic and political power of the LDCs and, by raising the stakes on specific economic issues, bring pressure on the DCs to take the steps necessary to maintain restrictive arrangements.

Whether this solution would be effective, however, is far from clear. Apart from the power that the DCs would have within the Common Fund, the weak link in the chain is the ability to make problems at the level of ICOs into major issues at the level of the Common Fund. Buffer stocks for copper, coffee, and perhaps tin might be so large that their failure would threaten the Common Fund. In these cases the pressures that could be brought to bear on the DCs would probably be very nearly irresistible. But the failure of an ICO in most commodities would not have this potential, and the ability of the Common Fund to stabilize the arrangement would be correspondingly limited.

Development of the IPC

This discussion points to a basic flaw in the design of the IPC. On the one hand, it is very likely that the individual ICOs would attempt to raise prices and that the Common Fund would be deeply involved with the resulting problems. On the other hand, the Common Fund does not have the means to deal effectively with the burdens that would be placed upon it. The IPC, consequently, would tend to be unstable and would be under pressure to evolve from its original form.

Although the way in which the IPC might develop cannot be predicted in any systematic way, it is possible to speculate based on the underlying problems, the structure of the IPC, and its objectives. The last is particularly important because it is likely to set the framework within which solutions are sought.

Resolution 93 (IV), adopted at UNCTAD IV, provides a reasonable indication of the expectations that the LDSs would bring to the IPC:

1. To achieve stable conditions in commodity trade, including avoidance of excessive price fluctuations, at levels which would:
   (a) be remunerative and just to producers and equitable to consumers;
   (b) take account of world inflation and changes in the world economic and monetary situations;
   (c) promote equilibrium between supply and demand within expanding world commodity trade;
2. To improve and sustain the real income of individual developing countries through increased export earnings, and to protect them from fluctuations in export earnings, especially from commodities.[20]

It seems obvious from this language that the reduction of price fluctuations is one objective. Beyond that, the LDCs hope to obtain through the IPC the funds necessary to speed the development of their economies.

Whether the IPC would have a significant impact on development is a major consideration. Suppose that the IPC operates smoothly. The price changes instituted by OPEC increased the oil suppliers' revenues by about $80 billion in each of 1974, 1975 and 1976. But increases in other commodity prices do not have anything like this potential. Exporting nations would no doubt find increased revenues helpful, but they would not be sufficient to permit the massive development programs undertaken by the Middle Eastern oil producers. Furthermore, although some of the LDCs would gain from increased commodity prices, many others would lose. Finally, simply reducing price fluctuations would not have a profound effect on the rate of growth in the LDCs as a group. The predictable result, then, even under favorable assumptions, would be frustrated expectations.

This point is not worth pursuing in isolation because the supposition that the IPC would operate smoothly is grossly unrealistic. Once it were instituted, the IPC would be faced with the problems identified earlier. Frustration over its limited results would appear as one major theme in a broader pattern of failures and disputes.

General dissatisfaction with the IPC, as well as some specific problems, would invariably give rise to pressures for reform of the system, especially of the Common Fund. First, problems that apparently call for the coordination of various commodity agreements would appear. For example, the ICOs that maintained buffer stocks would be in competition with diversification programs for a limited amount of funds. Other circumstances that would suggest a need for coordination can also be imagined (such as the impact of aluminum prices on the demand for copper).

Second, the failure of individual agreements or acute problems within ICOs would demonstrate the inadequacy of the Common Fund. The tin buffer stock provides an example. During 1958, the International Tin Agreement was purchasing in an effort to maintain price, while at the same time the U.S.S.R. increased its exports of tin. This problem was solved when buyers, especially the United Kingdom, imposed quotas in tin imports from the U.S.S.R.[21] Similarly, in the early 1960s, the buyers in the International Coffee Agreement, including the United States, limited imports from nonmember nations.[22] But such one-at-a-time responses are likely to be cumbersome and unsatisfactory. It is reasonable to expect, then, that the Common Fund would be under pressure to evolve toward a stronger and further-reaching form.

Once the objectives and logic of the IPC are accepted, arguments such as those just sketched would have substantial appeal. In fact, there is a sense in which they are correct. The IPC, as it is described in UNCTAD documents, would not live up to expectations. Over time, the Common Fund might evolve into an organization capable of maintaining prices above the competitive level. Or, as the lessons of history are relearned, the IPC might evolve into a system of pure buffer stocks, although this seems unlikely. Finally, the Common Fund might degenerate into insignificance or collapse under the weight of accumulated disputes.

Alternative Integrated Programs

Alternative integrated programs can be generated by removing the flaws in the IPC. One possibility is to perfect the IPC as a mechanism for transferring income via higher prices, which would require strengthening the Common Fund's means of coping with the forces set up by prices above the competitive level. Another is to design the ICOs so that prices are not increased above the competitive level, which would remove the underlying cause of the instability in the IPC. Organizations can be conceived along both of these lines.

The Commodity Price Authority

A question that has emerged is whether the use of price increases as a means of transferring income to the LDCs is a practical possibility. If this question is approached strictly in terms of economic mechanisms, the answer is a qualified "yes." The key to maintaining commodity prices above the competitive level would be a certificate system, which would deal directly with the problem of overshipping and, more important, would provide a means of limiting entry. If a certificate system was in force, potential entrants would have to apply to the ICO for membership and a share of the market. It is not realistic to suppose that an international agency could entirely exclude entry, but an ICO with a strong certificate system could effectively limit the rate of entry.[23]

The problem with the IPC as a means of raising prices, however, does not lie with its economic measures but rather with the balance of political forces. In particular, the arguments of the preceding section lead to the conclusion that the Common Fund would not entirely solve the problem of gaining the adherence of importing nations to restrictive commodity agreements.

Because the principle behind the Common Fund—the focusing of the power of the LDCs and raising the stakes to the level of North/South relations—is cogent, the solution would seem to lie in strengthening the Common Fund. It is possible to think of a variety of ways to do so, but in terms of the problems considered here, the obvious course would be for the Common Fund to absorb the individual ICOs. An arrangement of this sort is taken to be the Commodity Price Authority. There is no guarantee that a Commodity Price Authority could successfully maintain commodity prices above the competitive level. The problems of containing market forces are formidable, and the authority would not have any uniquely powerful means available. It would, however, have a better chance of gaining the adherence of importing nations to restrictive arrangements and, to this extent, would have much better prospects than past commodity agreements or the IPC.

These comments simply posit the existence of a Commodity Price Authority. When political forces are considered, there is a question as to whether a Commodity Price Authority could be created or, if it were created, would be stable.

The notion of a Commodity Price Authority involves (at least) three political contradictions. The first of these grows out of the fact that the DCs would be required to act against their own immediate economic interests. The assumption is that they would be held hostage by the economic and political power of the LDCs, which, oil aside, is not so. Even within the commodities trade, the balance of power runs in favor of the DCs, so they would have to act voluntarily against their own interests and domestic politics would probably preclude that.[24]

Second, it is by no means clear that a Commodity Price Authority would be to the political advantage of the DCs. The political gain usually posited is improved economic relations with the LDCs or, more generally, an organizational structure that promotes cooperative relations between the DCs and the LDCs. However, the Commodity Price Authority would be a regulatory authority, and the DCs would, through membership, be intimately involved in a variety of very painful situations. In effect, the DCs would assume the burden of policing world commodity trade, and, as the United States has learned to its sorrow, "the policeman's lot is not an happy one."

Third, the LDCs are likely to find the balance of power within a Commodity Price Authority unattractive. Under such an authority, many economic actions that individual LDCs might wish to undertake would be matters for negotiation and hence would be subject to a significant measure of control by the DCs. Furthermore, if and when the DCs took steps to maintain the Commodity Price Authority, they could be expected to insist on a corresponding degree of control. But such control would probably be intolerable to the LDCs and is the opposite of one of the results sought through the IPC.[25]

These comments do not stretch to a conclusive argument that using price increases to transfer income to the LDCs are a practicable impossibility. They do reinforce the impression left previously that efforts to maintain commodity prices above the competitive level would be very contentious and probably ineffective.

Buffer Stock Authority

The other alternative integrated program is a system of centrally financed buffer stocks. Moving in this direction from the IPC is a surgical process. The problem is not the Common Fund but the provisions of the individual ICOs, in particular, the extensive use of restrictions on supply envisioned by the IPC. To put this point in its strongest form, it is useful to assume that the Buffer Stock Authority would operate a system of buffer stocks. It would then differ from the Commodity Price Authority only in the use made of restrictions on supply.

Supply management measures are such an entrenched feature of international commodity agreements that their exclusion would be a radical step. For that reason, it is useful to ask if any controls on supply could be employed while preserving the essential features of a pure buffer stock. This is a question of safeguards.

The central difficulty is that the use of supply management measures can lead a buffer stock into price support activities. This would occur when the target price is set too high and the resulting excess supply, instead of being allowed to force price down, is choked off with export quotas and/or production controls. The buffer stock then ceases to be a device for limiting price fluctuations and, instead, becomes a way of supporting price above the long-run competitive level.

This sequence of events might be controlled via procedural safeguards: controls on exports or production should not be triggered automatically when market price falls below the floor price; and any export quotas or production controls that are imposed should automatically lapse after a relatively brief period. These safeguards would not prevent restrictions on supply from being used to increase price above the long-run equilibrium. Assuming the voting procedures typically specified in commodity agreements, they would simply give importing nations a veto over restrictions on supply.

It is conceivable that procedural safeguards would be sufficient but not be very satisfactory. There would be a tendency to attempt a compromise, particularly when suppliers are faced with the prospect of making painful, long-run adjustments. Therein lies a difficulty. Importing and exporting nations can compromise on prices, but they cannot compromise away the forces set up by a price above the competitive level. It is possible to draw a conceptual line between the use of supply management measures to limit short-run declines in price and the use of restrictions on supply to increase price above the competitive level. However, this distinction is very difficult to draw in concrete terms, and the history of commodity agreements provides no grounds for an optimistic appraisal of the ability of commodity agreements to manage restrictions on supply.

In addition to procedural safeguards, there are substantive restrictions on the use of supply management that could be written into an agreement. These could be entirely arbitrary. For example, the agreement could specify that exports could never be restricted to less than, say, 90 percent of the base and that quotas could be in effect only, say, one year in five. Alternatively, the use of supply management could be tied to the floor price. Suppose that the target price is set equal to a moving average of past market prices and that the floor price is 90 percent of the target price. If supply management measures were used to defend the target price, it would be of no consequence that the target price is set as a moving average of market prices. This possibility can be eliminated by adopting the following rules:

Rule 1. Restrictions on supply cannot be imposed if the market price is above the floor price.

Rule 2. If the use of restrictions on supply leads to a price above the floor price, then the restrictions on supply are automatically relaxed, and the floor price, rather than the actual market price, is used in computing the target price.

These rules guarantee that the target price will track the market price and, via rule 1, guarantee that supply controls would automatically lapse eventually. Hence, if the problem is to prevent a buffer stock from turning into a price raising mechanism, a refinement of both rules might be used in place of procedural safeguards.

These comments say nothing about why controls on supply should be used. As was pointed out in chapter 2, there is virtually no reason for using controls on supply if the purpose is simply to reduce period-to-period price fluctuations. In fact, considering both private and public costs, controls on supply are the least efficient of the available stabilization mechanisms. Hence, while some combination of substantive and procedural safeguards might be adequate to ensure that a buffer stock would not inadvertently lead into price-raising activities, there seems to be no reason to face the dangers and costs involved in the use of supply management.

Concluding Comments

There is a tendency to discuss the idea of a Common Fund or an integrated program without regard for the differences among the types of arrangements that are included under these general headings. To some extent this is fair enough because how commodity arrangements are designed would not affect the basic interests of importing and exporting nations and would not alter the array of political forces. However, taking these matters as given, the way in which commodity arrangements are structured does matter.

A system of pure buffer stocks related by a Common Fund would not involve any narrowly economic contradictions. The instability in such an arrangement would arise from a mismatch of economic consequences and the LDCs' expectations. Although a system of pure buffer stocks could reduce price fluctuations, this would not result in a transfer of resources to the LDCs and would not have a profound impact on the rate of growth in the LDCs.

A set of commodity agreements that attempted to increase prices would, like any other restrictive arrangement, be under continuous pressure from market forces. However, unlike restrictive ICOs, a Commodity Price Authority contains a coherent set of means for dealing with these problems and, like a set of pure buffer stocks, might be stable in terms of the economic forces involved. The sources of instability would arise at the political level. A Commodity Price Authority might be acceptable to the LDCs, but it would be a virtually impossible arrangement for the DCs.

The IPC contains elements of both of these cases in an uncomfortable way. In very broad terms, the flaw in the IPC lies in a mismatching of means and ends. It seems clear that the LDCs seek the IPC as a means of increasing commodity prices, but the means included in the IPC are insufficient to accomplish the task. Although a weak Common Fund might survive for many years as an essentially defunct organization, the LDCs' expectations would eventually be frustrated by what would be called a failure of the DCs' political will. This event and the process of an IPC's disintegration would be an important source of international acrimony.

Notes

1. UNCTAD, "Consideration of Issues Relating to the Establishment and Operation of a Common Fund," report by the Secretary-General of UNCTAD, TD/B/IPC/CF/2, November 10, 1976, pp. 7-8.

2. UNCTAD, "Common Fund: Mode of Operations," note by the UNCTAD Secretariat, TD/B/IPC/CF/L.5, January 15, 1977, pp. 6-7.

3. UNCTAD, "Consideration of Issues," p. 6, paragraph 21. See also UNCTAD, "Common Fund: Financial Requirements," note by the UNCTAD Secretariat, TD/B/IPC/CF/L.2, December 29, 1976, p. 15, paragraph 31.

4. UNCTAD, "Common Fund: Financing of Operations Other Than Stocking," note by the UNCTAD Secretariat, TD/B/IPC/CF/L.3, December 29, 1976, p. 5.

5. UNCTAD, "Consideration of Issues," p. 4, paragraph 12.

6. UNCTAD, "Common Fund: Decision Making and Management," note by the UNCTAD Secretariat, TD/B/IPC/CF/L.6, January 11, 1976, pp. 5-6.

7. See ibid. for a discussion of possible voting formulas.

8. UNCTAD, "An Integrated Programme for Commodities: Measures for Individual Commodities," report by the UNCTAD Secretariat, TD/B/C.1/194, October 1, 1975, pp. 56-59, 61-63.

9. Ibid., p. 7.

10. Ibid., p. 56. See also UNCTAD, "Copper: The Elements of an International Stabilization Arrangement," report by the UNCTAD Secretariat, TD/B/IPC/Copper/L.2, August 26, 1976, pp. 14-15.

11. UNCTAD, "An Integrated Programme," p. 23.

12. UNCTAD, "Elements of an International Agreement on Rubber," report by the UNCTAD Secretariat, TD/B/IPC/Rubber/L.2, December 17, 1976, pp. 13-14.

13. UNCTAD, "Elements of an International Agreement on Jute, Kinaf and Allied Fibres," report prepared jointly by the Secretariats of FAO and UNCTAD, TD/B/IPC/Jute/L.2, September 23, 1976, pp. 13-14.

14. UNCTAD, "Common Fund: Financing of Operations Other Than Stocking," note by the UNCTAD Secretariat, TD/B/IPC/CF/L.3, December 29, 1976, p. 5.

15. UNCTAD, *Proceedings of the United Nations Conference on Trade and Development, Second Session: Commodity Problems and Policies*, TD/97, vol. 2 (New York: United Nations, 1968), pp. 17-18.

16. J.M. Keynes, "The International Control of Raw Materials," *Journal of International Economics* 4 (1974):303, 306-311.

17. Indexation, which is implicitly favored by resolution 93 (IV), is one of the leading issues associated with the IPC. An index of the cost of producing the commodity might be used, but indexation would then merely refer to a formula for computing a target price equal to long-run average cost.

18. UNCTAD, "Consideration of Issues," p. 3, paragraphs 8-9.

19. An example is provided by a situation that occurred in the copper industry. On October 20, 1965, Chile forced an increase in the price of its copper to thirty-eight cents per pound. Most of Chile's output was produced by two U.S. firms–Kennecott Copper and the Anaconda Company–and sold in the United States. The increase in the Chilean price prompted an increase in the U.S. producers' price early in November, but the increase was shortly thereafter rescinded to conform with guidepost policy. The rollback put the U.S. producers in an awkward position because they were taxed in Chile on the basis of the Chilean price. "Three months later, in officially separate actions, Chile agreed to sell 100,000 tons in the U.S. at the producers' price of 36¢ and the U.S. government, through the Alliance for Progress agreed to lend Chile $10 million for forty years to use in copper development." Charles River Associates, *Economic Analysis of the Copper Industry* (Report to the Property Management and Disposal Service, General Services Administration, March 1970).

20. United Nations, Conference on Trade and Development, fourth session Nairobi, "Integrated Programme for Commodities," May 5, 1976, resolution 93 (IV).

21. J.W.F. Rowe, *Primary Commodities in International Trade* (Cambridge: Cambridge University Press, 1965), pp. 171-172.

22. Irving Kravis, "International Commodity Agreements to Promote Aid and Efficiency: The Case of Coffee," *Canadian Journal of Economics* 1 (1968):295-317.

23. Difficulties would still arise. Suppose, for example, that some country is a relatively new, low-cost cocoa producer that has been given only a small

quota. It might well decide to go into the chocolate business. Then, say, British chocolate producers would have to buy relatively high-cost cocoa while facing competition from low-price imports from that country. They are very likely to cry "foul."

24. Suppose, for example, that an ICO in copper succeeds in substantially increasing price, and, as a result, production is expanded and entry attracted. The initial response would be production controls. The United States now is the world's largest copper producer, and if production controls were to be effective, U.S. producers would have to be included. A visible, direct, and fairly immediate consequence would be unemployment of copper workers in the United States. Could any U.S. administration explain why it supports an international organization whose actions reduce employment while increasing prices paid by consumers?

25. There is also a real possibility that an IPC would increase the LDCs' dependence on commodities. To the extent that it creates additional profits, the IPC would promote diversification. The forces tending toward an increased or maintained reliance on commodities lie in the pattern of restrictions that would be associated with an effective IPC. Once an IPC was in place, entrants would face a pattern of production controls, export quotas, and limitations on entry enforced, via the ICOs, by the vested interests of existing suppliers. At a minimum, many of the LDCs would find their economic options reduced.

6 Options for Policy on Commodity Arrangements

The institutions that now mediate international trade were created by the Allies in the wake of World War II. The system was designed along liberal lines. Efforts were made to reduce barriers to trade, and financial arrangements were created to promote the flow of trade. In part, the postwar decisions responded to the experience of the 1930s when world markets were badly fractured by trade barriers and the international monetary system virtually collapsed, and in part to a belief that economic integration promotes mutual security.

During the postwar period per-capita income has increased rapidly in the DCs and more slowly in most of the LDCs. This fact alone would be sufficient to cause LDC leaders to question the way in which world trade is organized. A more pointed cause for criticism lies in the persistence of tariff and nontariff barriers, which limit the LDCs' opportunities for trade. From the LDCs' perspective, the world trading system does not look very liberal and, if twenty-five years of history are given any weight, the opportunities for reducing the barriers to trade that they face must seem bleak.

Through four successive UNCTADs, the LDCs have increasingly focused on commodity agreements as a means of obtaining offsetting advantages in commodity trade. The DCs have been in the position of responding to the LDCs' proposals, in particular, the Integrated Programme for Commodities (IPC). In the foreground of the issues posed by the IPC is the question of what types of commodity agreements are acceptable. Behind this is the question of how commodity agreements should be viewed in terms of development assistance, trade barriers, and other issues that divide the DCs and the LDCs. Both of these questions are set in the larger frame of the character of political relations between the DCs and the LDCs.

U.S. Policy on Commodity Arrangements

The United States has had a policy on commodity agreements since, at least, the years just after World War II.[1] Tracing the policy from that point might be of some interest, but for present purposes it is necessary only to look at U.S. policy on the IPC.

The IPC was effectively the subject of the Seventh Special Session of the U.N. General Assembly, held in September 1975. The U.S. position was stated in a speech by Secretary of State Henry Kissinger, which was thought at the time to be significantly more "responsive" and "constructive" than past U.S. positions. The United States did not accept the IPC, but it did accept some of the broad arguments behind it. It first agreed that development assistance programs have failed: "We have learned from experience that the methods of development assistance of the 1950s and 60s are no longer adequate." And it saw no prospect for increases in development assistance: "Realistically, we cannot expect the level [of development assistance] to increase significantly over the coming years. To put it frankly, the political climate for bilateral aid has deteriorated."[2] Because development assistance had played a major role in the past, this position opened the question of the future basis for international cooperation on development.

The United States effectively agreed that instability in prices and export earnings is a critical problem:

> The swings and shocks of economic adversity are a global concern tearing at the fabric of developed and developing nations alike. The cycle of good times and bad, abundance and famine, does vast damage to lives and economies. Unemployment, falling standards of living, and the ravages of inflation fuel social and political discontent. We have recently seen the corrosive effects in many countries.[3]

One of the major arguments behind the IPC is, of course, that instability in commodity prices and/or the LDCs' export earnings is a major obstacle to development and that international cooperation on development should accordingly be focused on the problems of the commodity markets.

Finally, the United States noticed the question of the balance of control in major international economic institutions: "The process of decision should be responsive to change. On many issues developing countries have not had a voice that reflects their role. This is now changing." It continued, "Basic economic realities, such as the size of economies, participation in world trade, and financial contributions, must carry great weight."[4] The U.S. position on control of international financial institutions was thus guarded but not closed.

Altogether, there was a fair measure of agreement between the IPC and the U.S. position on the legitimate areas of concern. The measures proposed by the United States, however, were sharply different from those included in the IPC. Without saying so explicitly, the United States rejected the IPC and presented its own counterplan.

The U.S. position on commodity arrangements as a means of stabilizing commodity prices was relatively simple: "Buffer stocks can be an effective technique to moderate instability in supplies and earnings. On the other hand, price-fixing arrangements distort the market, restrict production, and waste resources for everyone." Acceptance of the possibility of buffer stocks was a slight departure from earlier policy, but the United States took the position that "there is no simple formula that will apply equally to all commodities. The

United States therefore proposes to discuss new arrangements in individual commodities on a case by case basis."[5] This approach implied a rejection of the IPC, in that the IPC envisioned the simultaneous negotiation of a set of agreements. Furthermore, the United States took no notice of the idea of a Common Fund.

The United States distinguished instability in commodity prices from instability in the LDCs' earnings and placed major weights on the latter. Measures to stabilize commodity prices were rejected as a means of stabilizing export earnings. Instead, the United States proceeded directly from the argument that sharp drops in export earnings disrupt investment programs in the LDCs. The U.S. proposal was for what was called a Development Security Facility, to be located in the IMF, which would "give loans to sustain development programs in the face of export fluctuations; up to \$2.5 billion, and possibly more, in a single year and a potential total of \$10 billion in outstanding loans."[6] The Development Security Facility, a type of compensatory financing scheme, was apparently the specific counterproposal in the U.S. proposal to the Common Fund and, since the United States saw only a limited role for commodity agreements, to the problem of "stabilization."

The IPC relies principally on the stabilization of commodity prices, through commodity agreements, as a vehicle for accelerating the growth of the LDCs. In contrast, the United States took the position that prevention of sharp declines in the LDCs' export earnings is a precondition for growth to occur but is not itself a significant stimulus to growth. This position gives efforts to reduce declines in the LDCs' export earnings an important but not a preponderant role and implies that measures to accelerate the LDCs' growth must then be found elsewhere.

The United States maintained its position in favor of reductions in barriers to trade but stressed the role of private capital:

> The United States . . . believes it is time for the world community to address the basic requirements for accelerating growth in developing countries:
>
> – First, developing countries must have better access to capital markets.
> – Second, we must promote the transfer of technology.
> – Third, it is time to reach an international consensus on the principles to guide the beneficial operation of transnational enterprises.[7]

The U.S. statement proposed a number of initiatives under each of these headings, the most important of which were an expansion of the International Finance Corporation and the creation of an International Investment Trust to "mobilize portfolio capital for investment in local enterprises."[8] To summarize, the U.S. position on measures for accelerating the LDCs' growth advocated development assistance at roughly existing levels, reduction of trade barriers, and measures to increase the flow of private capital to the LDCs.

Altogether, the stance the United States adopted at the Seventh Special Session had a traditional shape.[9] The principal departure from its past positions lay in the proposed Development Security Facility, which responded in a major way to the LDCs' concern with instability in the export earnings. In this respect, the United States agreed, where it had not in the past, that measures directed to the problems of the commodity markets have a large role to play in international cooperation on development. However, it rejected commodity agreements as a means of transferring income to the LDCs, rejected the creation of a system of commodity agreements, and stressed reduction in trade barriers and increased flows of private capital as the principal means of accelerating the LDCs' development.

The U.S. position was taken, without fundamental changes, into UNCTAD IV, held in Nairobi during May 1976. It did not fare well. The major U.S. initiative, the International Resources Bank, was rejected and the plenary session of the conference adopted resolution 93 (IV), which set up a timetable for the creation of a Common Fund and eighteen individual commodity agreements.[10] Preliminary talks on the Common Fund began in September 1976.

The United States agreed to enter into the preparatory conferences on the Common Fund and then, in March 1977, into the negotiating conference on the Common Fund. At that time, it stated that it had no "prior objections" to a Common Fund but that it regarded powers, functions and structure of a Common Fund as open questions.[11] This represented a marked change in U.S. policy from its objections in principle to the idea of a Common Fund.

Participation in negotiations on the Common Fund implies that the United States would find some sort of integrated commodity program acceptable and so marks the end of the case-by-case approach. Entry into the Common Fund negotiations also seems to imply a shift in emphasis from trade and aid, which were the basis of U.S. policy in the past, to commodity arrangements. This is essentially a list of abandoned policy positions. The net result might be described as an open-minded attitude on commodity arrangements, but that is not a policy on what types of policy arrangements, if any, would be acceptable to the United States or a policy on the proper role of commodity agreements.

The Alternatives

It is tempting to approach the questions raised by the IPC by starting with the question of international cooperation on development and proceeding to an examination of development assistance programs, trade barriers, investment flows, and, perhaps, commodity agreements of various sorts. This pattern of thought (and especially the basic principles that it emphasizes) is relevant but cannot be brought to bear on the current issues in a straightforward way. The obstacle to doing so lies in the fact that the United States has agreed that commodity agreements of some unspecified sort would be acceptable. Consequently, the broader issues must be approached through policy on types of commodity arrangements.

Types of Commodity Arrangements

A discussion of alternative types of commodity arrangements must begin with the distinction between measures to increase the average level of commodity prices and measures to reduce period-to-period fluctuations in commodity prices. This distinction is obviously of direct importance to both importing and exporting nations, and it is also relevant to the efficiency with which resources are employed. Perhaps more important than either of these, the distinction between a reduction in price fluctuations and higher commodity prices has implications for the content of North/South relations. Measures to reduce fluctuations in commodity price and/or the LDCs' export earnings–buffer stocks and compensatory financing–need not involve any direct controls over importers or exporters. Measures to increase prices, however, require controls, particularly over the amount that can be produced and the right of entry into the commodity industries. The DCs, then, assume a regulatory role to the extent that they involve themselves in efforts to increase commodity prices.

The analysis from this point would be simple if the IPC were clearly designed to raise commodity prices, but the reality of the IPC is more subtle and complex. At the opening of the first negotiating session of the Common Fund, UNCTAD Secretary-General Gamani Corea characterized the overall form of the IPC as follows:

> Then again, it is sometimes said that the objective of the Integrated Programme is in one way or another to raise prices indiscriminately and thereby bring about income transfers from consuming to producing countries. But we have made it patently clear that the question of prices in regard to individual products would not be determined *a priori* in terms of the Integrated Programme in general. It would, on the contrary, be determined in the process of negotiations between producers and consumers in the context of negotiations for individual commodity arrangements.[12]

This description is accurate. The Common Fund outlined in UNCTAD documents would be essentially a financial institution and is adapted to raising the capital for buffer stocks. The International Commodity Agreements (ICOs) envisioned by UNCTAD, however, have the essential features of agreements designed to increase prices, and the arguments presented in chapter 5, lead to a strong presumption that the individual ICOs would attempt to hold prices above the competitive level.

The character of the IPC is probably best understood in terms of its evolution over a period of years. In the special circumstances that prevailed during the 1930s, commodity agreements enjoyed a limited measure of success, but the agreements that existed before and those that have existed since have not been successful. The arrangements envisioned by the IPC do not differ in any essential way from those of the past, and the underlying forces that have led to past failures remain undiminshed, so there is every reason to expect that the

IPC's commodity agreements would suffer the same instability that has affected past agreements. The Common Fund, of course, is unlike anything that has operated in the past, and it is possible to see in it the outline of a solution to the problems of past agreements. The Common Fund would focus the power of the LDCs and would not be lightly abandoned by the DCs. A Common Fund, might be able to pressure the DCs into taking the steps required to maintain individual restrictive arrangements. This, however, is not the most likely prospect. The Common Fund would inevitably be involved with the problems of the individual ICOs, but the powers and resources available to the Common Fund would probably not be sufficient to prop up failing agreements. As a result, there is a strong likelihood that the Common Fund would decay or eventually collapse under the burden of accumulated disputes.

The Common Fund is the most prominent aspect of the IPC, and, for that reason, there is a tendency to look to its provisions for ways of correcting the flaws in the IPC, but this is not the only possibility. At its roots, the problem with the IPC is a mismatching of means and ends: the Common Fund is adapted to financing buffer stocks while there is a reasonable expectation that the individual ICOs would attempt to maintain prices above the competitive level. The other plane on which a solution to the problems of the IPC could be sought, then, is to match appropriate means and ends.

One possibility is an organization, such as the Commodity Price Authority, designed to increase commodity prices. A second possibility is a program, including buffer stocks, that would be limited to reducing fluctuations in commodity prices and the LDCs' export earnings. Pushed to its limits, this is what has been called the Buffer Stock Authority.

The Buffer Stock Authority would make no use of controls on supply, which is the principal way in which it would differ from the Commodity Price Authority. Some use of restrictions on supply could be made while maintaining the essential features of a pure buffer stock, but if supply management measures are to be used at all, they must be subject to draconian procedural and substantive safeguards. The implication, then, is that the choice between raising price and reducing price fluctuations largely comes down to the policy on supply management measures.

The Role of Commodity Agreements

The issues raised by the IPC go beyond the prices of bananas and coffee and beyond even those of bauxite, copper, and iron. The LDCs regard the IPC as a major first step toward a restructuring of the international economic system and a means of significantly accelerating the pace of their development. Commodity agreements must consequently be appraised as part, and conceivably a predominant part, of economic relations with the LDCs. The issue posed by the

IPC, then, is not just commodity agreements but commodity agreements in relation to policies on trade, development assistance, and international economic institutions.

The IPC emerged from a period of twenty-five years in which international cooperation on development rested on development assistance and trade liberalization. Both of these are discounted in the thinking behind the IPC. The LDCs argue, and the DCs have agreed, that past development assistance programs have not succeeded and that funds allocated to development assistance are unlikely to be increased. On trade it is argued that tariff and nontariff barriers that discriminate against the LDCs are common, that there is little prospect that these barriers will be reduced, and, moreover, that the LDCs might not benefit by a regime of free trade.

In place of "trade and aid," the IPC would directly intervene in the commodity markets via commodity agreements and a Common Fund. Just how far an IPC along the lines suggested by the UNCTAD Secretariat would go in displacing established policies and institutions is not clear, but the possibilities can be outlined.

The clearest of these is the implications of the IPC for the conditions of trade in commodities. Commodity agreements under an IPC would probably evolve into "orderly marketing arrangements" (an extensive system of export and/or production controls as well as import quotas). Then instead of moving in the direction of reducing trade barriers, an IPC such as that outlined in UNCTAD documents would extend and systematize nontariff barriers to trade in commodities.

The implication of an IPC for development assistance programs is not so clear. Documents describing the IPC have stated that it is not intended to be a substitute for existing development assistance programs. However, the LDCs and some DCs regard the IPC as a way of transferring resources to the LDCs, and if commodity agreements are accepted as a means of making transfers to the LDCs, it is difficult to believe that existing development programs could retain any vitality.

These points do not do full justice to the possible scope of an IPC. The IPC is presented as a flexible organizational structure that can and should evolve over time in response to problems that arise: "It is desirable that, in the establishment of a new institution, its purposes should be formulated in such a way that they do not impede the development of its role in the light of experience and changing circumstances."[13] From this point of view, the crucial aspect of an IPC would be a commitment by the DCs to work through its structure, especially the Common Fund, to deal with the problems of development. The Common Fund would assume a paramount role in international cooperation on development. Various specialized agencies of the U.N., the World Bank, and the General Agreement on Tariffs and Trade would not disappear, but they presumably would be reduced to a secondary order of importance.

A system of pure buffer stocks related by a Common Fund need not challenge existing policies on development assistance and trade liberalization. More important, a system of pure buffer stocks or, more generally, measures to reduce fluctuations in commodity prices and the LDCs' export earnings would probably not have a large impact on development and so could not bear the burden of being the principal instrument of international cooperation on development.

One option would be to accept a system of pure buffer stocks and simply maintain the status quo on development assistance and efforts to reduce barriers to trade. This would to only a very limited extent constitute an initiative on economic development, and if that is desired, a system of pure buffer stocks must be coupled with other measures.

The number of alternatives is limited. Although development is an extremely complex process, its sine qua non is real investment. This requires foreign exchange, which the LDCs can obtain from three sources: earnings from exports, especially exports of commodities; bilateral and multilateral development assistance; and the private capital markets, which include loans and direct private foreign investment. If price increases are ruled out as a mechanism of making transfers, the broad alternatives are direct transfers, the reduction of barriers to trade, and measures designed to increase flows of private capital to the LDCs.

Initiatives in these areas might be linked to the acceptance of a system of pure buffer stocks strictly on a policy level. Thus, no institutional link would be established between the Common Fund and other programs. Alternatively, a Common Fund and pure buffer stocks for various commodities might be made part of a larger institution. This option might be viewed as a matter of restructuring and consolidating various existing programs, with the addition of a system of pure buffer stocks.

The benefits of buffer stocks in several commodities might well exceed their costs, but it seems unlikely that the creation of a system of buffer stocks would have a profound effect on the LDCs' development. This leads back to the point of departure. There is a consensus among economists that the most efficient ways for the DCs to redeem their commitment to aid the LDCs lie in a reduction in barriers to trade and development assistance. One commentator has observed that the proper response to critics of foreign aid is that "it has never seriously been tried."[14] Commodity agreements might, then, be rejected entirely and "trade and aid" accepted as the basis for international cooperation on development.

To summarize, the following policy packages have been mentioned:

1. An IPC along the lines suggested by UNCTAD, which would tend to displace existing programs.
2. A system of pure buffer stocks, related by a Common Fund, with or without initiatives on trade, aid, and investment.

3. Commodity agreements on a case-by-case basis, with or without initiatives on trade, aid, and investment.
4. Rejection of commodity agreements, including buffer stocks, with or without any initiatives on trade, aid, and development.

The role that is granted to commodity agreements decreases from point 1 to 4, and there is a major discontinuity between alternative 1 and alternative 2. Commodity agreements are taken in the IPC to be the major vehicle for attacking the problems of economic development. This view (at least by intent) is rejected in the remaining alternatives in which buffer stocks are understood as limited, specialized devices that might be useful in reducing price fluctuations but that should not be used to transfer income to the LDCs. Under points 2-4, the major burden of international cooperation on development would fall on trade, aid, and investment.

A Sample Program

The movement in U.S. policy has been from the fourth of these alternatives toward the second. It may then be useful, as a way of summarizing the issues, to elaborate an extreme version of this option. The program to be considered involves the creation of a single institution (the Agency), which would be made up of four separate funds:

Commodity Funds

1. A stabilization fund, divided into two parts: a buffer stock authority, which would finance and operate buffer stocks, and a buffer fund authority, which would provide compensatory financing for commodities for which a buffer stock is uneconomical.
2. A diversification fund.

Development Funds

3. A development assistance fund, which would make grants, as well as loans, on concessional terms.
4. A commercial loan facility.

The Agency's diversification fund is assumed to be essentially the same as that included in the Common Fund, but its stabilization fund is very different from the corresponding parts of the IPC. First, where the Common Fund would finance only buffer stocks run by ICOs, the Agency would bypass the creation of organizations for individual commodities and operate buffer stocks. But the Agency's buffer stocks would make no use of controls on supply, while the IPC's commodity agreements would to a large extent be supply management arrangements. Second, the Agency's buffer fund would provide compensatory financing. Compensatory financing is one of the measures considered in the IPC, and in several cases, UNCTAD reports state that compensatory financing should be part of the arrangement adopted. Nevertheless, the IPC and, especially, the Common Fund do not contain any new compensatory financing mechanism.

Existing institutions contain more or less close counterparts to each of the Agency's funds, which raises the question of why there is a need for a new institution or a reorganization of existing institutions.[15] The principal argument made—and one that lies at the heart of the case for the IPC—is that existing institutions do not deal adequately with the problems of instability in commodity prices and the LDCs' export earnings. The available evidence leaves room for skepticism about the extent to which instability in their export earnings is an obstacle to the LDCs' development. However, as such, the position that steps are required to stabilize the LDCs' export earnings is not particularly controversial.

The discussion then drops down to the plane of choice among stabilization mechanisms. Commodity agreements would be the principal vehicle of the IPC, with compensatory financing used as a supplementary measure. At the Seventh Special Session, the United States suggested that primary weight be placed on compensatory financing, with buffer stocks assigned a secondary role. By making a place for both compensatory financing and buffer stocks, the Agency carries forward this dispute.

One of the questions posed by the Agency's stabilization fund is, Which is the more economical means of limiting declines in the LDCs' export earnings: compensatory financing or buffer stocks? The analysis of this question in chapter 2 led to the conclusion that neither mechanism dominates the other in terms of benefits and costs; compensatory financing can be better for some commodities, and buffer stocks better for others. However, the available evidence tends to favor (pure) buffer stocks for the ten core commodities in the IPC. For some of these commodities, it appears that a given transfer can be made at lower capital cost through a buffer stock, while in other cases the direct benefits to reducing price seem to be large enough to offset the larger capital costs of buffer stocks.

A buffer stock, however, would not necessarily be limited to reducing period-to-period price fluctuations. Under the pressure of events, a buffer stock might be led by flaws in its own rules into an attempt to maintain price above the long-run competitive equilibrium. Furthermore, there is strong support from the LDCs and some of the DCs for the use of commodity agreements as a means of transferring income to the LDCs via higher prices.

A discussion of the proper role of buffer stocks involves the question of whether price increases should be used to make transfers to the LDCs. The United States has consistently rejected the use of commodity agreements as a transfer mechanism. If this policy is accepted, the question is how, if it is possible at all, to ensure that a buffer stock could be limited to the task of reducing price fluctuations.

The solution adopted in the specification of the Agency is a complete prohibition on the use of supply management measures. If controls on supply cannot be imposed and continual purchases are impossible because of budget limitations, a buffer stock could not maintain price above the competitive level. Rules, of course, can change, and suppliers have a persistent interest in higher prices. Then, whether buffer stocks would tend to evolve into restrictive arrangements remains a question.

No less important are the allocation problems posed by the Agency. It is far from clear which of the LDCs are most seriously affected by instability in export earnings. Given the limitations on the use of buffer stocks, this would be a key question in the allocation of capital between the buffer stock authority and the buffer fund authority. It is also not clear how the magnitude of the effects of instability in export earnings compares with the difficulties of making long-run adjustments, and this comparison would govern the allocation of resources between the stabilization and the diversification funds.

The broader allocation problem posed by the Agency is that of the distribution of resources between the commodity funds and the development funds. Existing research indicates that instability in export earnings is a severe problem for perhaps a majority of the LDCs, but the magnitude of the problem has not been fully characterized. Consequently, the extent to which development strategy should be focused on reducing fluctuations in the LDCs' export earnings remains largely a matter of judgment. The IPC is more or less explicitly understood as an alternative to development assistance. Hence, the inclusion of development assistance funds in the Agency and the prohibition on the use of supply management represent a strategy for international development efforts that is very different from that embodied in the IPC.

At this point the Agency comes into conflict with a basic part of the motivation behind the IPC. As indicated earlier, much of the force behind the IPC derives from the ineffectiveness of past development assistance programs and the lack of progress on reducing barriers to trade. The Agency would be prohibited from using supply management measures, so it could not provide restrictions on trade that favor the LDCs to offset existing restrictions that work to their disadvantage, and the Agency would make transfers directly rather than via price increases. The Agency, then, would involve a continued or renewed commitment to trade and aid as the major elements of international cooperation on development.

These comments point to a broad difference in conception between the IPC and the Agency. The Common Fund and the individual ICOs are seen as flexible, cooperative structures through which problems can be solved as they arise. The Agency is, instead, conceived as a set of specialized measures, each tailored to a particular type of problem. The commodity funds are designed to deal with some problems of the commodities markets, while the weight of international cooperation on development is placed on the development assistance funds. Within the first of these categories, the stabilization funds are assigned the task of reducing short-run fluctuations in commodity prices and the LDCs' export earnings, while the task of easing long-run transitions would be assigned to the diversification fund.

It is best to admit that narrowly economic considerations do not argue strongly for or against combining commodity funds and development assistance funds in a single organization. The Agency should instead be understood as pointing to the problem involved in making changes that respond to the LDCs' legitimate concerns without placing undue weight on commodity arrangements or abandoning existing policies on trade liberalization.

Concluding Comments

Perhaps the pivotal question raised in this discussion is whether commodity agreements should be used as a flexible, cooperative mechanism or designed for specific, limited purposes. The first of these implies an open-ended commitment to work through commodity arrangements to attack the problems of development; the latter would lead to the use of pure buffer stocks and compensatory financing to reduce fluctuations in commodity prices and the LDCs' export earnings.

The results of this study run strongly against the idea that commodity arrangements can or should be used as a flexible, problem-solving instrument. A commodity agreement is overtly a cooperative venture, but so is marriage, and the analogy is appropriate. How a system of commodity agreements would work out would depend largely on how the system is set up and what burdens are placed on it.

Notes

1. See Edward S. Mason, *Controlling World Trade* (New York: McGraw-Hill, 1946), for a discussion of commodity issues and policy problems in the immediate postwar period. Of particular interest is a proposal for a policy on commodity agreements along the lines of chapter VI of the Havana Charter advanced by the U.S. Department of State. See ibid., pp. 252-262.
2. Henry Kissinger, "Global Consensus and Economic Development," *U.S. Department of State Bulletin* 73 (September 22, 1975):427, 430.
3. Ibid., p. 427.
4. Ibid., p. 440.
5. Ibid., p. 437.

6. Ibid., p. 429.
7. Ibid., p. 430.
8. Ibid.
9. The U.S. statement to UNCTAD I pointed to the limitations of development assistance and stressed the role of private investment. See UNCTAD, *Trade and Development: Policy Statements*, E/CONF. 46/141, vol. 2 (New York: United Nations, 1964), pp. 394-399, esp. p. 397. The U.S. statement to UNCTAD II also stressed the role of private investment in development. See UNCTAD, *Proceedings of the United Nations Conference on Trade and Development, Second Session: Report and Annexes*, TD/97, vol. 1 (New York: United Nations, 1968), pp. 189-192, esp. p. 192.
10. The International Resources Bank was conceived primarily as an intermediary between the private capital markets and the LDCs. See Kissinger, "UNCTAD IV," pp. 5-6.
11. See statement of Deputy Assistant Secretary of State Stephen Bosworth to the opening session of the first negotiating conference to the Common Fund, processed, March 10, 1977.
12. UNCTAD, "Report of the First Preparatory Meeting for the Negotiation of a Common Fund," TD/B/IPC/CF/4, December 22, 1976, annex 1, pp. 7-8.
13. UNCTAD, "Consideration of Issues Relating to the Establishment and Operation of a Common Fund," report by the Secretary-General of UNCTAD, TD/B/IPC/CF/2, November 10, 1976, paragraph 19, p. 5.
14. G.K. Helleiner, *A World Divided* (Cambridge: Cambridge University Press, 1976), p. 2.
15. The International Monetary Fund has a compensatory financing facility and a facility for financing buffer stocks. The European Economic Community has also recently instituted a compensatory financing arrangement called STABEX. The Agency's communication loan fund parallels the IBRD. There are, of course, many development assistance programs.

Appendix A: Computation of the Numerical Examples

This appendix describes the procedures and assumptions used in obtaining the values shown in tables 2-7, 3-4, 3-5, and 4-1.

Computation of Direct Benefits and Costs

The values shown in table 3-4 were computed using results derived by B.F. Massell, "Price Stabilization and Welfare," *Quarterly Journal of Economics* 83 (1969):285-298. Massell assumes that supply and demand are, respectively, described by

$$q^s = \alpha P + x, \tag{A.1}$$

$$q^d = -\beta P + y, \tag{A.2}$$

where x and y are "shift factors." He then computes

$$\bar{G}_s = \frac{(\alpha + 2\beta)\sigma_{xx} - \alpha\sigma_{yy}}{2(\alpha + \beta)^2}, \tag{A.3}$$

$$\bar{G}_c = \frac{(2\alpha + \sigma\beta)\sigma_{yy} - \beta\sigma_{xx}}{2(\alpha + \beta)^2}, \tag{A.4}$$

where $\bar{G}_s$ and $\bar{G}_c$ are, respectively, the expected gains from price stabilization to sellers and buyers, and σ_{xx} and σ_{yy} are the variance of x and the variance of y.

Multiplying and dividing by $(P/q)^2$, A.3 and A.4 can be rewritten as

$$\bar{G}_s = \left[\frac{(\eta_s - 2\eta_d)\sigma_{xx} - \eta_s\sigma_{yy}}{2(\eta_s - \eta_d)^2}\right]\frac{P}{q}, \tag{A.5}$$

$$\bar{G}_c = \left[\frac{(2\eta_s - \eta_d)\sigma_{yy} + \eta_d\sigma_{xx}}{2(\eta_s - \eta_d)^2}\right]\frac{P}{q}, \tag{A.6}$$

where η_s and η_d are, respectively, the elasticity of supply and the elasticity of demand.

Equations A.5 and A.6 were used to compute the values presented in table 3-4. Crude estimates of σ_{xx} were obtained by assuming that supply is 10 percent above its base level, as measured by $\overline{q}$, one-third of the time, 10 percent below base one-third of the time, and at its base level one-third of the time. Given these assumptions, $\sigma_{xx} = (0.66 \times 10^{-2})\overline{q}^{-2}$. A value for σ_{yy} was computed similarly. The values used for η_s, η_d, $\overline{P}$, and $\overline{q}$ are those shown in table A-1. The elasticities of supply and demand for cocoa, coffee, tea, wool, cotton, wheat, rice, and sugar were computed using results contained in F.G. Adams, "An Econometric Model of the World Sugar Market," University of Pennsylvania, Department of Economics, Discussion Paper No. 330 (October 1974) and F.G. Adams and J. Behrman, "Seven Models of International Commodity Markets," unpublished manuscript prepared for the United Nations Conference on Trade and Development, December 1974. The elasticities for copper were taken from F. Fisher, P. Cootner, and M. Baily, "An Econometric Model of the World Copper Industry," *Bell Journal of Economics* 3, no. 2 (Autumn 1972). In the remaining cases (jute, sisal, rubber, and tin) the elasticities used were elicited from commodity experts. Prices were obtained from the International Bank for Reconstruction and Development, *Commodity Trade and Price Trends* (1975). The prices used were seven-year moving averages ending in the last year reported for all commodities except copper, which was an eight-year moving average. The quantities are estimates for 1971 computed from data provided by the same source.

Computation of Buffer Stock Capital Requirements

Denote by $\overline{P}$ the target price and by P'' and P', respectively, the upper and lower prices that are to be defended. Let f be the fraction by which price is permitted to vary from $\overline{P}$. The floor and ceiling prices are then $P' = (1 - f)\overline{P}$ and $P'' = (1 + f)\overline{P}$, respectively. Assume that supply and demand are, respectively, described by

$$q^s = \alpha(1 \pm h) + \beta P, \tag{A.7}$$

$$q^d = a(1 \pm g) + bP, \tag{A.8}$$

where g and h are shift variables. A positive value for h shifts supply to the right, and a negative value shifts supply to the left. Similarly, a positive value for g shifts the demand curve up, and a negative value shifts the demand curve down.

Denote by z^* maximum buffer stock purchases required to defend P'. Maximum purchases must be made when supply is at its maximum level and demand is at its minimum level. Therefore, z^* is described by

$$a(1 - g) + b(1 - f)\overline{P} + z^* = \alpha(1 + h) + \beta(1 - f)\overline{P}. \tag{A.9}$$

Table A-1
Values Used in the Computation of the Numerical Examples

Commodity	*Elasticity of Supply*	*Elasticity of Demand*	*Base Production*	*Price*
Cocoa	0.34	−0.32	3.488 million l.t.	$ 821.43/l.t.
Coffee	.33	−.27	66.319 million bags	$ 53.50/bag
Tea	.31	−.16	1.244 million m.t.	$ 690.18/m.t.
Cotton	.71	−.27	11.324 million m.t.	$ 526.10/m.t.
Sugar	.22	−.16	71.4 million m.t.	$ 253.96/m.t.
Jute	.30	−.50	0.722 million m.t.	$ 326.30/m.t.
Sisal	.15	−.30	0.385 million m.t.	$ 466.00/m.t.
Rubber	.15	−.40	2628.4 million kg	$ 0.55/kg
Copper	.22	−.14	7.975 million m.t.	$ 1112/m.t.
Tin	.10	−.08	0.206 million m.t.	$ 4950.8/m.t.
Wool	.25	−.24	9.742 million m.t.	$1550.00/m.t.
Wheat	.71	−.20	321.3 million m.t.	$ 73.21/m.t.
Rice	.20	−.06	187.3 million m.t.	$ 109.77/m.t.

Expanding this expression:

$$\{a + b\bar{P}\} - ag - bf\bar{P} + z^* = \{\alpha + \beta\bar{P}\} + ah - \beta f\bar{P}. \tag{A.10}$$

Each of the bracketed terms is equal to $\bar{q}$, so

$$z^* = (ag + ah) + f(b - \beta)\bar{P}. \tag{A.11}$$

Dividing by $\bar{q}$ gives

$$\nu^* = \frac{(ag + \alpha h)}{\bar{q}} + (\eta_d - \eta_s)f, \tag{A.12}$$

where $\nu^* = z^*/\bar{q}$ is the maximum annual increment to the buffer stock as a fraction of base production, and η_d and η_s are, respectively, the elasticities of demand and supply. The value of the stock is $\bar{P}z^*$.

The values of the intercepts were computed as

$$\alpha = \bar{q}(1 - \eta_s), \tag{A.13}$$

$$a = \bar{q}(1 - \eta_d), \tag{A.14}$$

which hold given equations A.7 and A.8.

It was assumed in computing the benefit measures that appear in table 3-4 that the variation in supply, given stable demand, yields a ±10 percent variation in output from the base; and similarly, given stable supply, variations in demand produce ±10 percent variation from base in output. Straightforward manipulations of equations A.7 and A.8 give the values of g and h corresponding to these assumptions as

$$g = 0.1^* \left\{ 1 - \left[\frac{(1 - \eta_s)\eta_d}{(1 - \eta_d)\eta_s} \right] \right\}, \tag{A.15}$$

$$h = 0.1^* \left\{ 1 - \left[\frac{(1 - \eta_d)\eta_s}{(1 - \eta_s)\eta_d} \right] \right\}. \tag{A.16}$$

Substituting these expressions, and the expressions for the intercepts, into equation A.12 and simplifying gives

$$\nu^* = - \left[\frac{(\eta_d - \eta_s)^2}{\eta_s \, \eta_d} \right] {}^*0.1 + (\eta_d - \eta_s)f. \tag{A.17}$$

Equation A.17 was used to compute the capital requirements shown in table 3-5. The values used in the computations were those given in table A-1.

Computation of the Ratio of Increased Revenues to Suppliers to Buffer Stock Expenditures

Let P' be the floor price and P_o be the price in the absence of buffer stock purchases, and assume that $P' > P_o$. Assuming that all purchases are made at the floor price, buffer stock expenditure, E, is

$$E = P'(q_s' - q_d'), \tag{A.18}$$

where q_s' and q_d' are, respectively, quantity supplied and quantity demanded at P'. The increase in revenue caused by the buffer stock purchases, ΔR, is

$$\Delta R = P'q_s' - P_o q_s^o, \tag{A.19}$$

where q_s^o is quantity supplied at P_o.

The difference between increased revenues and expenditures reduces to

$$\Delta R - E = P'q_d' - P_o q_s^o. \tag{A.20}$$

Price and quantity demanded can be expressed as

$$P' = P_o + \Delta P, \tag{A.21}$$

$$q_d' = q_d^\circ + \Delta q. \tag{A.22}$$

Substitute these relationships into equation A.20 and note that $q_s^\circ = q_d^\circ = q^\circ$. Then, on simplification and rearrangement, A.20 yields

$$\Delta R - E = (1 + \eta_d)\Delta P q^\circ + \Delta P \Delta q, \tag{A.23}$$

where η_d is the elasticity of demand. Division by E gives on rearrangement

$$\frac{\Delta R}{E} = 1 + (1 + \eta_d)(1 - P_o/P')\left(\frac{q^\circ}{z}\right) + \left(\frac{\Delta P}{P'}\right)\left(\frac{\Delta q}{z}\right), \tag{A.24}$$

where $z \equiv q_s' - q_d'$ is buffer stock purchases.

Note that $\Delta q = \eta_d \dfrac{\Delta P}{P'} q^\circ$ and define $k \equiv 1 - P^\circ/P'$. Equation A.24 can be rewritten as

$$\frac{\Delta R}{E} = 1 + k\,\{1 + \eta_d + \eta_d k q^\circ/z\}\,. \tag{A.25}$$

Given the assumptions made earlier on the magnitude of shifts in supply and demand, $q_o = \bar{q}$, equation A.25 gives

$$\frac{\Delta R}{E} = 1 + k\{\,1 + \eta_d(1 + k/v)\,\}. \tag{A.26}$$

The minimum price without buffer stock purchases, P_o, and $\bar{P}$ are respectively described by

$$a(1 - g) + bP_o = \alpha(1 + h) + \beta P_o, \tag{A.27}$$

$$a + b\bar{P} = \alpha + \beta\bar{P}, \tag{A.28}$$

which imply

$$(\beta - b)(\bar{P} - P_o) = \alpha h + ag. \tag{A.29}$$

Substituting the expressions for α, h, a, and g given earlier, equation A.29 yields on simplification:

$$(\beta - b)(\bar{P} - P_{\circ}) = -\left[\frac{(\eta_d - \eta_s)^2}{\eta_s - \eta_d}\right] 0.1*\bar{q}. \tag{A.30}$$

Multiplying and dividing the left-hand side of this expression by $\bar{P}/\bar{q}$,

$$(\eta_s - \eta_d)\bar{q}\frac{(\bar{P} - P_{\circ})}{\bar{P}} = -\left[\frac{(\eta_d - \eta_s)^2}{\eta_s - \eta_d}\right] 0.1\, q\text{, or,} \tag{A.31}$$

$$\frac{\bar{P} - P_{\circ}}{\bar{P}} = \left[\frac{1}{\eta_s} - \frac{1}{\eta_d}\right] 0.1. \tag{A.32}$$

Substituting $\bar{P} = (\frac{1}{1-f})P'$ into A.32 yields on rearrangement

$$1 - P_{\circ}/P' = 1 - (\frac{1}{1-f})\left\{1 - (\frac{1}{\eta_s} - \frac{1}{\eta_d})0.1\right\}. \tag{A.33}$$

The values in table 2-6 were computed using equations A.17 and A.33, evaluated for $f = 0.1$, and equation A.26. In all cases, the elasticities given in table A-1 were used, which is to assume that the elasticities do not change appreciably over the range of prices considered.

Computation of the Effects of a Price Increase on Production, Revenue, and Profit

This section develops the formulas used to compute the estimates presented in table 4-1. Production and price are denoted by q and P, respectively. Revenue is denoted by R and the elasticity of demand by η_d.

From the definition of elasticity of demand,

$$\Delta q \doteq \eta_d q h \tag{A.34}$$

where $h = \Delta P/P$. The incremental revenue is

$$\Delta R \doteq (1 + 1/\eta_d)P\Delta q. \tag{A.35}$$

Substituting the expression on the right-hand side of A.34 for Δq and simplifying gives

$$\Delta R \doteq (1 + \eta_d)hR. \tag{A.36}$$

The change in profit is

$$\Delta\Pi \doteq \Delta R - \Delta C, \qquad \text{(A.37)}$$

where C is total cost. Assume that long-run average cost is a constant $\overline{C}$ and that the initial price $\overline{P}$ is equal to $\overline{C}$. Then

$$\Delta C = \overline{C}\Delta q = \overline{P}\Delta q \doteq \eta_d hR, \qquad \text{(A.38)}$$

again using A.34. Substituting equations A.36 and A.38 into A.37:

$$\Delta\Pi \doteq hR. \qquad \text{(A.39)}$$

Equations A.36 and A.39 were used to compute the values shown in table 4-1. The elasticities used are given in table A-1.

Appendix B: Resolution of the UNCTAD

Distr.
GENERAL

TD/RES/93(IV)
10 June 1976

Original: ENGLISH

United Nations Conference on Trade and Development

Fourth session
Nairobi, 5 May 1976
Agenda item 8

RESOLUTION ADOPTED BY THE CONFERENCE

93(IV). Integrated Programme for Commodities[1/]

The United Nations Conference on Trade and Development,

Recalling the Declaration and the Programme of Action on the Establishment of a New International Economic Order[2/] as well as the Charter of Economic Rights and Duties of States,[3/] which lay down the foundations of the new international economic order, General Assembly resolution 623 (VII) of 21 December 1952 and Conference recommendation A.II.1.

Recalling, in particular, section I, paragraph 3(a) (iv), of the Programme of Action on the Establishment of a New International Economic Order, relating to the preparation of an over-all integrated programme for "a comprehensive range of commodities of export interest to developing countries",

Recalling also section I, paragraph 3, of General Assembly resolution 3362 (S-VII) of 16 September 1975, which states, inter alia, that "an important aim of the fourth session of the United Nations Conference on Trade and Development, in addition to work in progress elsewhere, should be to reach decisions on the improvement of market structures in the field of raw materials and commodities of export interest to the developing countries, including decisions with respect to an integrated programme and the applicability of elements thereof",

---

1/ The Conference adopted this resolution without dissent.

2/ General Assembly resolutions 3201 (S-VI) and 3202 (S-VI) of 1 May 1974.

3/ General Assembly resolution 3281 (XXIX) of 12 December 1974.

GE.76-66135

Taking note of the work undertaken on commodities in preparation for the fourth session of the Conference, in particular the proposals submitted by the Secretary-General of UNCTAD for an integrated programme for commodities.

Reaffirming the important role of UNCTAD in the field of commodities,

Bearing in mind resolution 16 (VIII) of the Committee on Commodities concerning decisions by the Conference at its fourth session with respect to an integrated programme for commodities, on, *inter alia*:

(a) objectives;

(b) commodities to be covered;

(c) international measures;

(d) follow-up procedures and time-table for the implementation of agreed measures;

Affirming the importance to both producers and consumers, notably the developing countries, of commodity exports for foreign exchange earnings and of commodity imports for welfare and economic development,

Recognizing the need to conduct international trade on the basis of mutual advantage and equitable benefits, taking into account the interests of all States, particularly those of the developing countries,

Recognizing also the need for improved forms of international co-operation in the field of commodities which should promote economic and social development, particularly of the developing countries,

Recognizing further the urgent need for substantial progress in stimulating food production in developing countries and the important bearing of international commodity policies on this aim,

Recalling the proposal in the Manila Declaration and Programme of Action for the establishment of a common fund for the financing of international commodity stocks, co-ordinated national stocks or other necessary measures within the framework of commodity arrangements,4/

Bearing in mind the view that there might be financial savings in operating a central facility for the purpose of financing buffer stocks,

Taking note of the readiness of a number of countries, expressed prior to and at the fourth session of the Conference, to participate in and financially support a common fund,

Noting that there are differences of views as to the objectives and modalities of a common fund,

---

4/ TD/195, part two, section one, paragraph 5(a).

Convinced of the need for an over-all approach and an integrated programme for commodities which is a programme of global action to improve market structures in international trade in commodities of interest to developing countries, and which is consistent with the interests of all countries, particularly those of the developing countries, and assures a comprehensive view of the various elements involved while respecting the characteristics of individual commodities,

Decides to adopt the following Integrated Programme for Commodities:

I. OBJECTIVES

With a view to improving the terms of trade of developing countries and in order to eliminate the economic imbalance between developed and developing countries, concerted efforts should be made in favour of the developing countries towards expanding and diversifying their trade, improving and diversifying their productive capacity, improving their productivity and increasing their export earnings, with a view to counteracting the adverse effects of inflation, thereby sustaining real incomes. Accordingly the following objectives are agreed:

1. To achieve stable conditions in commodity trade, including avoidance of excessive price fluctuations, at levels which would:
   - (a) be remunerative and just to producers and equitable to consumers;
   - (b) take account of world inflation and changes in the world economic and monetary situations;
   - (c) promote equilibrium between supply and demand within expanding world commodity trade;
2. To improve and sustain the real income of individual developing countries through increased export earnings, and to protect them from fluctuations in export earnings, especially from commodities;
3. To seek to improve market access and reliability of supply for primary products and the processed products thereof, bearing in mind the needs and interests of developing countries;
4. To diversify production in developing countries, including food production, and to expand processing of primary products in developing countries with a view to promoting their industrialization and increasing their export earnings;

5. To improve the competitiveness of, and to encourage research and development on the problems of, natural products competing with synthetics and substitutes, and to consider the harmonization, where appropriate, of the production of synthetics and substitutes in developed countries with the supply of natural products produced in developing countries.

6. To improve market structures in the field of raw materials and commodities of export interest to developing countries.

7. To improve marketing, distribution and transport system for commodity exports of developing countries, including an increase in their participation in these activities and their earnings from them.

II. COMMODITY COVERAGE

The commodity coverage of the Integrated Programme should take into account the interests of developing countries in bananas, bauxite, cocoa, coffee, copper, cotton and cotton yarns, hard fibres and products, iron ore, jute and products, manganese, meat, phosphates, rubber, sugar, tea, tropical timber, tin, and vegetable oils, including olive oil, and oilseeds, among others, it being understood that other products could be included, in accordance with the procedure set out in section IV below.

III. INTERNATIONAL MEASURES OF THE PROGRAMME

1. It is agreed that steps will be taken, as described in section IV, paragraphs 1 to 3, below, towards the negotiation of a common fund.

2. It is also agreed to take the following measures, to be applied singly or in combination, including action in the context of international commodity arrangements between producers and consumers, in the light of the characteristics and problems of each commodity and the special needs of developing countries:

(a) Setting up of international commodity stocking arrangements;

(b) Harmonization of stocking policies and the setting up of co-ordinated national stocks;

(c) Establishment of pricing arrangements, in particular negotiated price ranges, which would be periodically reviewed and appropriately revised, taking into account, *inter alia*, movements in prices of imported manufactured goods, exchange rates, production costs and world inflation, and levels of production and consumption;

(d) Internationally agreed supply management measures, including export quotas and production policies and, where appropriate, multilateral long-term supply and purchase commitments;

(e) Improvement of procedures for information and consultation on market conditions;

(f) Improvement and enlargement of compensatory financing facilities for the stabilization, around a growing trend, of export earnings of developing countries;

(g) Improvement of market access for the primary and processed products of developing countries through multilateral trade measures in the multilateral trade negotiations, improvement of schemes of generalized preferences and their extension beyond the period originally envisaged, and trade promotion measures;

(h) International measures to improve the infrastructure and industrial capacity of developing countries, extending from the production of primary commodities to their processing, transport and marketing, as well as to the production of finished manufactured goods, their transport, distribution and exchange, including the establishment of financial, exchange and other institutions for the remunerative management of trade transactions;

(i) Measures to encourage research and development on the problems of natural products competing with synthetics and consideration of the harmonization where appropriate, of the production of synthetics and substitutes in developed countries with the supply of natural products produced in developing countries;

(j) Consideration of special measures for commodities whose problems cannot be adequately solved by stocking and which experience a persistent price decline.

3. The interests of developing importing countries, particularly the least developed and the most seriously affected among them, and those lacking in natural resources, adversely affected by measures under the Integrated Programme, should be protected by means of appropriate differential and remedial measures within the Programme.

4. Special measures, including exemption from financial contributions, should be taken to accommodate the needs of the least developed countries in the Integrated Programme for Commodities.

5. Efforts on specific measures for reaching arrangements on products, groups of products or sectors which, for various reasons, are not incorporated in the first stage of application of the Integrated Programme should be continued.

6. The application of any of the measures which may concern existing international arrangements on commodities covered by the Integrated Programme would be decided by governments within the commodity organizations concerned.

IV. PROCEDURES AND TIME-TABLE

1. The Secretary-General of UNCTAD is requested to convene a negotiating conference open to all members of UNCTAD on a common fund no later than March 1977.

2. The Secretary-General of UNCTAD is further requested to convene preparatory meetings prior to the conference referred to in paragraph 1 above concerning, _inter alia_:

(a) Elaboration of objectives;

(b) The financing needs of a common fund and its structure;

(c) Sources of finance;

(d) Mode of operations;

(e) Decision-making and fund management.

3. Member countries are invited to transmit to the Secretary-General of UNCTAD, prior to 30 September 1976, any proposals they may have concerning the above and related issues.

4. The Secretary-General of UNCTAD is further requested to convene, in consultation with international organizations concerned, preparatory meetings for international negotiations on individual products, in the period beginning 1 September 1976. These meetings should complete their work as soon as possible, but not later than February 1978. The task of the preparatory meetings shall be to:

(a) Propose appropriate measures and techniques required to achieve the objectives of the Integrated Programme;

(b) Determine financial requirements resulting from the measures and techniques proposed;

(c) Recommend follow-up action required through the negotiation of commodity agreements, or other measures;

(d) Prepare draft proposals of such agreements for the consideration of governments and for use in commodity negotiating conferences.

5. The Secretary-General of UNCTAD is further requested to convene, as and when required, commodity negotiating conferences as soon as possible after the completion of each preparatory meeting held pursuant to paragraph 4 above. These negotiations should be concluded by the end of 1978.

6. The Secretary-General of UNCTAD is requested to undertake the necessary arrangements for the servicing of the preparatory meetings and the subsequent commodity negotiating conferences, in co-operation with the secretariats of the specialized commodity bodies and other organizations concerned.

7. It is agreed that international negotiations or renegotiations on individual commodities covered by existing agreements shall be in accordance with appropriate established procedures for the purpose of concluding international arrangements.

8. The Trade and Development Board is instructed to establish an ad hoc intergovernmental committee to co-ordinate the preparatory work and the negotiations, to deal with major policy issues that may arise, including commodity coverage, and to co-ordinate the implementation of the measures under the Integrated Programme.

145th plenary meeting
30 May 1976

Bibliography

Adams, F. Gerard. "An Econometric Model of the World Sugar Market." Discussion paper no. 330. Philadelphia: University of Pennsylvania, Department of Economics, October 1974.

_______, and Behrman, Jere. "Seven Models of International Commodity Markets." Report to the United Nations Conference on Trade and Development, December 1974.

Asher, Robert E. *Development Assistance in the Seventies.* Washington, D.C.: The Brookings Institution, 1970.

Balassa, Bela, and Associates. *The Structure of Protection in Developing Countries.* Baltimore: Johns Hopkins University Press for the International Bank for Reconstruction and Development and the Inter-American Development Bank, 1971.

Bauer, P.T. *The Rubber Industry.* Cambridge, Mass.: Harvard University Press for the London School of Economics and Political Science, 1948.

Baumol, William. "Speculation, Profitability and Stability." *Review of Economics and Statistics* 39 (1957):263-271.

Behrman, Jere. "Monopolistic Cocoa Pricing." *American Journal of Agricultural Economics* 50 (February 1968):702-719.

Bergsten, C. Fred. "The Threat from the Third World." *Foreign Policy* 11 (1971):102-124.

Bilder, Richard B. "The International Coffee Agreement: A Case History in Negotiation." *Law and Contemporary Problems* 28 (Spring 1963):328-391.

Carey, John, ed. *Law and Policy-Making for Trade Among "Have" and "Have-Not" Nations.* Dobbs Ferry, N.Y.: Oceana Publication, Inc., for the Association of the Bar of the City of New York, 1968.

Charles River Associates, "Public and Private Stockpiling for Future Shortages." Report to the National Commission on Supplies and Shortages, August 1976.

_______. "Economic Issues Underlying Supply Access Agreements: A General Analysis and Prospects in 10 Mineral Markets." Report to the U.S. Department of Labor, Bureau of International Labor Affairs, July 1975.

_______. *Economic Analysis of the Copper Industry.* Report to the Property Management and Disposal Service, General Services Administration, March 1970.

Commodities Research Unit, Ltd. *Co-ordinated National Stockpiles as a Market Stabilizing Mechanism–Copper.* London and New York: Commodities Research Unit, Ltd., 1977.

Cooper, Richard N. "A New International Economic Order for Mutual Gain." *Foreign Policy* 26 (Spring 1977):65-120.

Coppock, Joseph D. *International Economic Instability.* New York: McGraw-Hill, 1962.

Davis, Joseph S. "Experience Under Intergovernmental Commodity Agreements, 1902-1945." *Journal of Political Economy* 54 (1946):193-220.

DeVries, Barend A. *Export Experiences of Developing Countries.* World Bank Staff occasional paper no. 3. Washington, D.C.: International Bank for Reconstruction and Development, 1967.

Erb, Guy F., and Shiavo-Campo, Salvatore. "Economic Instability, Level of Development and Economic Size of Less Developed Countries." *Bulletin of the Oxford University Institute of Economics and Statistics* 31 (1969):263-283.

Evans, John W. *The Kennedy Round in American Trade Policy.* Cambridge: Harvard University Press, 1971.

Fisher, Franklin M.; Cootner, Paul; and Baily, N. Martin. "An Econometric Model of the World Copper Industry." *Bell Journal of Economics* 3 (Autumn 1972):568-609.

Frank, I. "The Role of Trade in Development." In R. Gardner and M. Millikan, eds. *The Global Partnership: International Agencies and Economic Development.* New York: Praeger, 1968.

Friedman, Milton. *Essays in Positive Economics.* Chicago: University of Chicago Press, 1953.

Gold, Gerald. *Modern Commodity Futures Trading.* 7th ed. New York: Commodity Research, Inc., 1975.

Gwyer, G.D. "Three International Commodity Agreements: The Experience of East Africa." *Economic Development and Cultural Change* 21 (October 1972):465-476.

Helleiner, G.K., ed. *A World Divided.* Cambridge: Cambridge University Press, 1976.

International Labor Office. *Intergovernmental Commodity Control Agreements.* Montreal: International Labor Office, 1943.

Johnson, Harry G. "Destabilizing Speculation: A General Equilibrium Approach." *Journal of Political Economy* 84 (1976):109-122.

_______. *Economic Policies Towards Less Developed Countries.* Washington, D.C.: The Brookings Institution, 1967.

_______. *The World Economy at the Crossroads.* Oxford: Oxford University Press, 1965.

Keynes, J.M. "The International Control of Raw Materials." *Journal of International Economics* 4 (1974):299-315.

_______. "The Policy of Government Storage of Foodstuffs and Raw Materials," *Economic Journal* 45 (1938):449-460.

Kissinger, Henry. "UNCTAD IV: Expanding Cooperation for Global Economic Development." U.S. Department of State, Bureau of Public Affairs, May 6, 1976.

_______. "Global Consensus and Economic Development." *U.S. Department of State Bulletin* 73 (September 22, 1975):425-441.

Knorr, K.E. *Tin Under Control.* Stanford, Calif.: Stanford University Food Research Institute, 1945.

Knudsen, Odin, and Parnes, Andrew. *Trade Instability and Economic Development.* Lexington, Mass.: Lexington Books, 1975.

Kravis, Irving. "International Commodity Agreements to Promote Aid and Efficiency: The Case of Coffee." *Canadian Journal of Economics* 1 (1968):295-317.

Krumme, Robert D. "International Commodity Agreements: Purpose, Policy, Procedure." *The George Washington University Law Review* 31 (April 1963):784-811.

Law, Alton D. *International Commodity Agreements.* Lexington, Mass.: Lexington Books, 1975.

League of Nations. Economic Committee. *Commercial Policy in the Post-War World.* Geneva: League of Nations, 1945.

Levin, Jonathan V. *The Export Economies.* Cambridge: Harvard University Press, 1960.

MacAvoy, P.W., and Pindyck, R.S. *The Economics of the Natural Gas Shortage.* Amsterdam: North-Holland Publishing Company, 1975.

McBean, Alasdair, I. *Export Instability and Economic Development.* Cambridge: Harvard University Press, 1966.

McIntyre, Alister. *Current Problems of Economic Integration: The Effects of Reverse Preferences on Trade Among Developing Countries.* United Nations Conference on Trade and Development. New York: United Nations, 1974.

McKinnon, R.I. "Futures Markets, Buffer Stocks, and Income Stability for Primary Producers." *Journal of Political Economy* 65 (1967):844-861.

McNicol, David. "The Two Price Systems in the Copper Industry." *Bell Journal of Economics* 6 (Spring 1975):50-73.

Maizels, A. "Review of Export Instability and Economic Growth." *American Economic Review* 58 (June 1968):575-580.

Mason, Edward S. *Controlling World Trade.* New York: McGraw-Hill, 1946.

Massell, B.F. "Some Welfare Implications of International Price Stabilization." *Journal of Political Economy* 68 (1970):404-417.

_______. "Price Stabilization and Welfare." *Quarterly Journal of Economics* 83 (1969):285-298.

_______; Pearson, S.R.; and Fitch, J.B. "Foreign Exchange and Economic Development: An Empirical Study of Selected Latin American Countries." *Review of Economics and Statistics* 54 (1972):208-212.

Michaely, Michael. *Concentration in International Trade.* Amsterdam: North-Holland Publishing Company, 1962.

Michels, Rudolf K. *Cartels, Combines and Trusts in Post-War Germany.* New York: Columbia University Press, 1928.

Mikdashi, Z. "Collusion Could Work." *Foreign Policy* 14 (Spring 1974):59-65.

Mintz, Ilse. *U.S. Import Quotas: Costs and Consequences.* Washington, D.C.: American Enterprise Institute, 1973.

Patinkin, Don. "Multi-plant Firms, Cartels, and Imperfect Competition." *Quarterly Journal of Economics* 61 (February 1947):173-205.

Pincus, John. *Trade, Aid and Development.* New York: McGraw-Hill, 1967.

Pindyck, Robert. "Gains to Producers from Cartilization of Exhaustible Resources." Working paper MITEL 76-012 WP. Massachusetts Institute of Technology, Energy Laboratory World Oil Project, May 1976.

Plummer, Alfred. *International Combines in Modern Industry.* London: Sir Isaac Pitman and Sons, 1938.

Political and Economic Planning Committee. *Atlantic Tariffs and Trade.* London: Allen and Unwin, 1962.

Rangarajan, C., and Sundararajan, V. "Impact of Export Fluctuations on Income–A Cross-Country Analysis." *Review of Economics and Statistics* 58 (August 1976):368-372.

Rowe, J.W.F. *Primary Commodities in International Trade.* Cambridge: Cambridge University Press, 1965.

Sidjanski, Dusan. *Current Problems of Economic Integration: The Role of Institutions in Regional Integration Among Developing Countries.* United Nations Conference on Trade and Development, TD/4/422, New York: United Nations, 1974.

Sorenson, Vernon L. *International Trade Policy: Agriculture and Development.* East Lansing: Division of Research, Graduate School of Business Administration, Michigan State University, 1975.

Stigler, G., and Kendahl, J. *The Behavior of Industrial Prices.* New York: National Bureau of Economic Research, 1970.

Stocking, George W., and Watkins, Myron W. *Cartels in Action.* New York: The Twentieth Century Fund, 1947.

Strauss, Frederick. "Report on the United Nations Conference on Trade and Development." Mimeographed. U.S. Department of Commerce, Bureau of International Commerce, July 1964.

Turnovsky, Stephen J. "The Distribution of the Welfare Gains from Price Stabilization: The Case of Multiplicative Disturbances." *International Economic Review* 17 (1976):133-148.

United Nations. *Official Records of the General Assembly Special Session.* New York: United Nations, 1976.

United Nations Conference on Trade and Development. "Common Fund: Mode of Operations." Note by the UNCTAD Secretariat. TD/B/IPC/CF/L.5, January 15, 1977.

_______. "Common Fund: Decision Making and Management." Note by the UNCTAD Secretariat. TD/B/IPC/CF/L.6, January 11, 1977.

_______. "Common Fund: Financial Requirements." Note by the UNCTAD Secretariat. TD/B/IPC/CF/L.2, December 29, 1976.

_______. "Common Fund: Financing of Operations Other Than Stocking." Note by the UNCTAD Secretariat. TD/B/IPC/CF/L.3, December 29, 1976.

_______. "Elements of an International Agreement on Rubber." Report by the UNCTAD Secretariat. TD/B/IPC/Rubber/L.2, December 17, 1976.

_______. "Report of the First Preparatory Meeting for the Negotiation of a Common Fund." TD/B/IPC/CF/4, December 22, 1976.

_______. "Consideration of Issues Relating to the Establishment and Operation of a Common Fund." Report by the Secretary-General of UNCTAD. TD/B/IPC/CF/2, November 10, 1976.

_______. "Elements of an International Agreement on Jute, Kinaf and Allied Fibres." Report prepared jointly by the Secretariats of FAO and UNCTAD. TD/B/IPC/Jute/L.2, September 23, 1976.

_______. "Copper: The Elements of an International Stabilization Arrangement." Report by the UNCTAD Secretariat. TD/B/IPC/Copper/L.2, August 27, 1976.

_______. "An Integrated Programme for Commodities: Measures for Individual Commodities." Report by the UNCTAD Secretariat, TD/B/C.1/194, October 1, 1975.

_______. *Proceedings of the United Nations Conference on Trade and Development, Third Session: Report and Annexes.* TD/180, vol. 1, New York: United Nations, 1973.

_______. *Proceedings of the United Nations Conference on Trade and Development, Second Session: Report and Annexes.* TD/97, vol. 1, New York: United Nations, 1968.

_______. *Proceedings of the United Nations Conference on Trade and Development, Second Session: Commodity Problems and Policies.* TD/97, vol. 2, New York: United Nations, 1968.

_______. *Trade and Development: Final Act and Report.* E/CONF. 46/141, vol. 1, New York: United Nations, 1964.

_______. *Trade and Development: Policy Statements.* E/CONF. 46/141, vol. 2, New York: United Nations, 1964.

_______. *Trade and Development: Commodity Trade.* E/CONF. 46/141, vol. 3, New York: United Nations, 1964.

United States. Congress. *Report by Congressional Advisors to UNCTAD IV.* Washington, D.C.: Government Printing Office, 1976.

_______. International Trade Commission. "International Commodity Agreements." Report by the U.S. International Trade Commission to the Subcommittee of International Trade of the Senate Committee on Finance. Washington, D.C.: Government Printing Office, 1975.

_______. Treasury. *U.S. Commodity Policy.* Washington, D.C.: Office of Raw Materials and Oceans Policy, Treasury Department, February 1976.

Walker, Herman. "The International Law of Commodity Agreements." *Law and Contemporary Problems* 28 (Spring 1963):392-415.

Wall, David. *The Third World Challenge: Preferences for Development.* London: The Atlantic Trade Study, 1967.

Wallace, Benjamin B., and Edminster, Lynn R. *International Control of Raw Materials.* Washington, D.C.: The Brookings Institution, 1930.

Walter, Ingo. "Barriers to International Competition: The Application and Liberalization of Nontariff Distortions." In *The United States and International Markets,* edited by Robert G. Hawkins and Ingo Walter. Lexington, Mass.: Lexington Books, 1972.

Wickizer, V.D. *Coffee, Tea and Cocoa.* Stanford, Calif.: Stanford University Press, 1951.

Worchester, Dean A., Jr. "Why 'Dominant Firms' Decline." *Journal of Political Economy* 65 (1957):338-346.

Yates, P. Lamartine. *Commodity Control.* London: Jonathan Cape, 1943.

Index

About the Author

David L. McNicol did his undergraduate work in economics at Harvard College and was awarded a masters degree in management and a doctorate in economics and finance in 1968 and 1973, respectively, by the Massachusetts Institute of Technology. While in graduate school, he was employed by Charles River Associates, where his work was primarily concerned with the construction of econometric models of the metals industries. Since then he has been on the faculties of the University of Pennsylvania and the California Institute of Technology and has served on the Senior Staff of the President's Council of Economic Advisors.